auschenberg exhib
Köln a couple of y
ery cool.
don't think that
oming to NY. I
o DC for 4 days
must return to CA
lass again. This
ews but surely I w
oming your way
ometime soon. Y
lways welcome

white
fish
press

A DIVISION OF 3 A.M. PRODUCTIONS
NEW YORK – CHICAGO – PORTAGE – EAST LANSING

ISBN 0-9667097-6-4

MIDNIGHT MIND NUMBER TWO *or* THE GUIDE TO SAFE CAMPING
COPYRIGHT ©2001 WHITE FISH PRESS/MIDNIGHTMIND.COM

ALL RIGHTS RESERVED.
PRINTED IN THE UNITED STATES OF AMERICA
LIBRARY OF CONGRESS CATALOGING-IN-PUBLICATION DATA ON FILE

PLEASE VISIT US ONLINE AT WHITEFISHPRESS.COM

WHITE FISH PRESS
PO BOX 1131
NEW YORK, NY 10003

FIRST PRINTING, SEPTEMBER 2001

PHOTOGRAPHY ON PAGES 9, 75, 103, 123, 131 BY DENNIS KWESELL

PHOTOGRAPHY THAT INCLUDES RELATIVES OF THE EDITOR ON PAGE 117.

NOTE ON THE REST OF THE ARTWORK: MOST OF THE IMAGES WERE EITHER CREATED FOR THIS PUBLICATION OR WERE OLD PHOTOS FOUND OVER THE YEARS WHICH ARE NOW PART OF THE WHITE FISH PRESS PHOTO COLLECTION AND MAY NOT BE REUSED WITHOUT WRITTEN PERMISSION FROM WHITE FISH PRESS. OR WE STOLE THEM IN WHICH CASE, YOU MAY USE THEM ALL YOU WANT. MOST OF WHAT WE STOLE IS FROM *The Boy Scout Handbook* WHICH MIGHT GO AGAINST EVERYTHING THE BOOK TEACHES YOU, AND WE ARE SORRY.

THIS BOOK IS BEST ENJOYED IN A TENT, READ BY FLASHLIGHT (PREFERABLY ONE THAT YOU HAVE TO HIT EVERY FEW MINUTES TO KEEP WORKING).

Exchange Policy
WILL WILL PROVIDE A NEW COPY OF MM#2 IF YOUR BOOK IS EATEN BY YOUR DOG. IN ORDER TO CLAIM YOUR NEW BOOK YOU MUST PROVIDE;

1. PROOF THAT IT WAS A DOG THAT ATE YOUR BOOK.
2. PROOF THAT IT WAS YOUR DOG.
3. WHAT IS LEFT OF YOUR BOOK MUST BE SENT TO US. (UNLESS YOUR DOG HAS DIGESTED THE BOOK.)
4. THE DOG'S NAME.

PLEASE NOTE: YOU MAY ONLY RETURN YOUR COPY ONCE. IF YOUR DOG EATS THE BOOK A SECOND TIME, YOU SHOULD NOT OWN A DOG.

PLEASE ALSO NOTE: WE LOVE DOGS AND THAT IS WHY WE OFFER THIS EXCHANGE POLICY. PLEASE DO NOT MAKE YOUR DOG EAT OUR BOOK AS THAT IS NOT FUNNY UNLESS WE ARE THERE TO SEE AND WE AREN'T. SO DON'T.

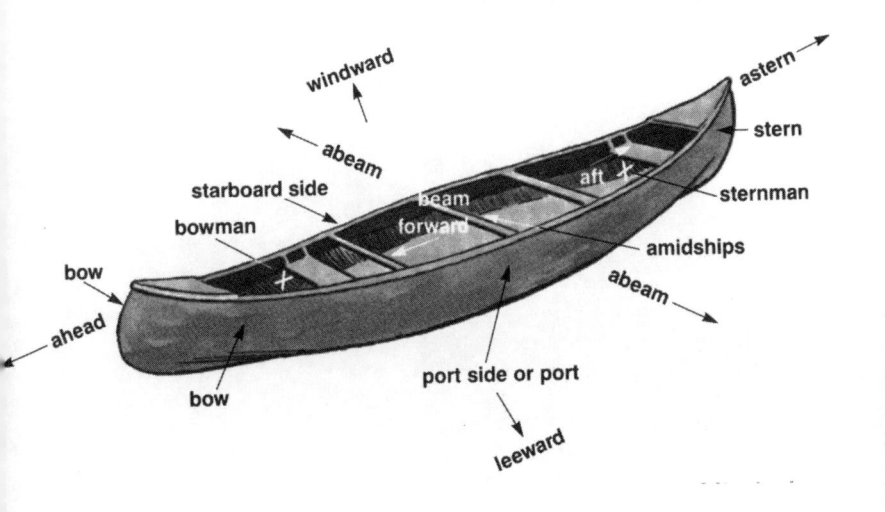

MIDNIGHT MIND NUMBER TWO
THE GUIDE TO SAFE CAMPING

GENERAL EDITOR/PUBLISHER
BRETT VAN EMST

COPY EDITOR
LAFCADIO GURN

MIDNIGHT MIND JOURNAL ADVISORY BOARD
JENNIFER CAYEA
SALLY DAYTON
EDWARD SERKEN
TOM SHORT
MARIKA STRUIK

THIS IS FOR THE BOTTOM FIVE

THE PLACES WHERE TRAILS DO NOT EXIST ARE NOT WELL MARKED.
— *from a comment card left for the U.S. Forest Service*

Table of Contents

Fiction

Sean Sullivan
The Intervention — PAGE 15

Kristina Neihouse
Squall — PAGE 37

Camping Tip #1 - The Two Types of Camping — PAGE 43

Non-Fiction

Linda Fasano List
Key West: The Peaceable Kingdom — PAGE 49

Camping Tip #2 - Camping Soundtrack — PAGE 55

Poetry

Jeff Mann
Mallory Square — PAGE 61

Cristina Perissinotto
Of Bikes and Lovers — PAGE 65

Christian Langworthy
Fossil — PAGE 71
Prints — PAGE 72

Marie Bahlke
Memory — PAGE 77
Going to Mendon in October — PAGE 78
Pacifist — PAGE 80

Marion Boyer
Tobacco Farmer's Wife — PAGE 85
Losing Faith — PAGE 86

Angela Mazaris
Autumn Baby — PAGE 91

John Grey
Shipwreck in the Reef — PAGE 95
Sunset Celebration — PAGE 96

Louis S. Faber
To a Poet, To the West — PAGE 101

Sarah Browning
Florida — PAGE 105

Dianalee Velie
When I Leave Your House — PAGE 111
Orchard Beach — PAGE 112
Unnecessary Junk — PAGE 114

Mary-Alice Herbert
Fantasy Fest (The Morning After) — PAGE 119

Daniel Spinella
Edison's First Film — PAGE 125
Galway Bay — PAGE 126
A Note from Emma Hutchinson to Col. Cody Concerning the 1,000-Mile Cowboy Race — PAGE 128

Jeff Vande Zande
Sundown — PAGE 133
In the Basement — PAGE 134
We Watched, We Waited — PAGE 136

Camping Tip #3 - Good *vs*. Bad   PAGE 139

AND ONE INTERVIEW...
Behind the Mind of Chris Dombrowski   PAGE 143
Interviewed by Julie Dunn.

Submission Policy   PAGE 148
Editor's Note   PAGE 149
Glossary of Terms   PAGE 154

A NOTE ON THE PHOTOGRAPHER...

DENNIS KWESELL

WE ASKED DENNIS IF HE HAD TIME TO WRITE A SHORT BIO. HE REPLIED, "TIME? IT'S ALL WE REALLY HAVE. AND STILL—EVERY MORNING—I HIT THE SNOOZE BUTTON 2 OR 3 TIMES.

FICTION

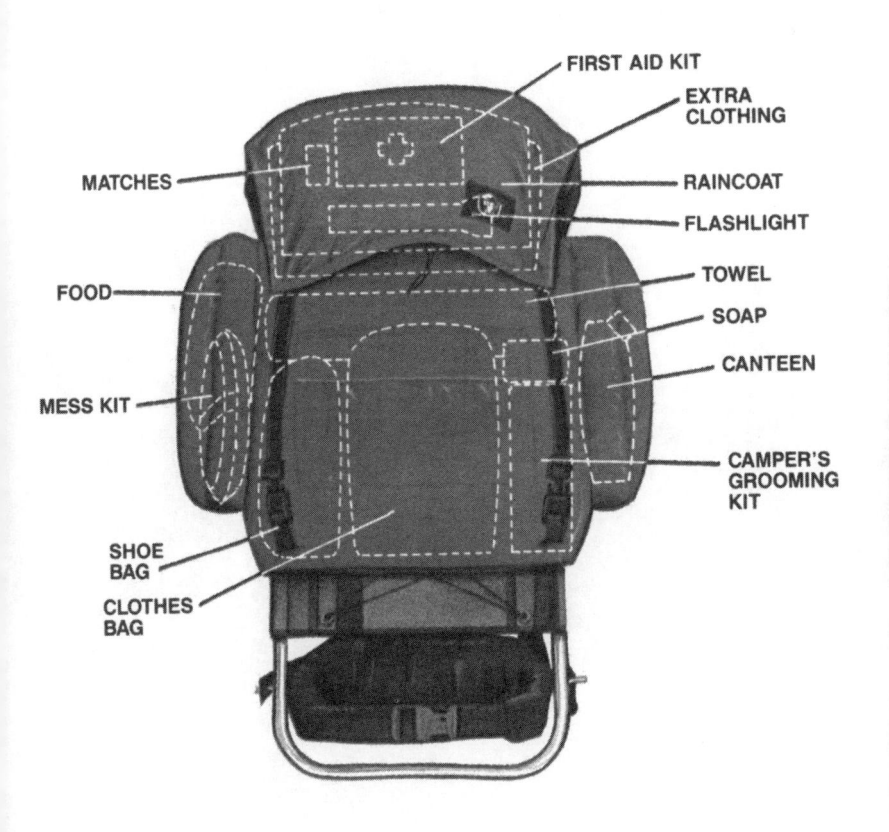

The Intervention
by Sean Sullivan

Sean Sullivan

Sean Sullivan grew up in Minnesota and now lives in New York City.

The Intervention

I meet myself in an East Village bar. It is Saturday afternoon and the place is quiet. There are two bikers playing pool. For a moment I think I've stood myself up, but then I spot me in a corner booth half-hidden by two leather jackets bullying a frail silver coat rack. The other me is sporting aviator shades and a black tuxedo, looking as though he has just stepped from the set of a secret agent film where he played, perhaps, the well-dressed villain, who at point blank range could only hit the hero in the arm. He is alone in the booth, dusting the tabletop with his hand.

"What's he having?" I ask the bartender.

"Scotch," he replies, "been here half the day."

I note the subject's moving lips, listless movements, and the way he seems too content with the dusting of the tabletop. "Two beers. Whatever you have on draft." The clicking of the billiard balls goes on behind me. As I pay for the drinks, I see my own reflection in the mirror behind the bar, and cannot keep from sizing up the seated me.

We are physically identical—the sharp nose, the weak chin; but even in that split second, I sense a pulse of intimidation from the other's aura. Oh, mercy. Ces't moi. My legs are a bit weak as I step back from the bar with the drinks in my hand.

How does one perform an introduction to one's self? We have all envisioned it at one time or another—in hazy pre-sleep wanderings, moments of deep spiritual evaluation, or even in the throes of a rare brand of narcissism. When magazines poll readers about whom in the world they would most like to meet, Jesus Christ and Adolf Hitler finish near the top. I think people fail to consider the most intriguing option. It has been said that we know ourselves the least. Conversely, it has been said that we only know ourselves. Usually the truth lies somewhere in the middle, but in this case I suspect that one or the other is indisputably correct. I have no idea which.

I approach the table wondering if he is watching me through those dark shades, but he gives no indication of this as he ushers another line of invisible crumbs over the table's edge. I set the drinks down firmly, hoping he will speak first. He stops dusting the tabletop, reaches up and elegantly adjusts the glasses on his nose. An earthquake comes. It is a horrible vibration—the repellant force of two similarly charged particles. It's as though gravity itself has got drunk. Now I am shaking, and not only from nerves. I try to stare at him but cannot. I sit down to keep from falling.

"Have a seat," he says, the voice familiar. "Excuse me." And with that, he stands and walks toward the men's room, leaving me awestruck and silent, alone in the booth. As he brushes by, I physically shudder. A mechanical wind pushes me three inches across my bench and up against the cold brick wall.

Let me explain how I was given this opportunity to meet myself. It was not by way of magic porthole, nor is it some literary hallucination. It is not a dream. You see, I have this habit of leaving myself messages on my own answering machine. Oftentimes, returning home from work to my voice mail, I hear myself reminding me to meet a friend somewhere for dinner or to take the garbage down in the morning. Sometimes I instruct myself to wear a suit the next day, because I have an out-of-office meeting.

Last Friday evening I came home to three messages. I was heating water for pasta as they played. The first reminded me to call my mother and the second chastised me for forgetting to pre-register to vote. By the third message the water was boiling and I could not make out the words, but my voice sounded formal and a little urgent and I froze at the sound of it. I had not remembered making this call. I turned off the stove and walked over to my machine. I hit play, erased the first two messages and sat down on the couch to listen to the third.

"Hi, it's you. Listen: It's time we speak. The indecision has become chronic. Admit it. Meet me at Doc Holliday's Bar at 1 o'clock tomorrow. It's time to let the pressure out. Okay? And don't think too much. Just be there."

I played the message all night long. I got drunk. I went through all the possible logical explanations. Was this the practical joke of some twisted friend? No. The recognition of one's own voice is achieved by so much more than mere sound: the speed of speech, the pauses, the choice of words. The invisible attitude makes it unmistakable. Had I myself left this message in some caffeine-induced moment of corporate exhaustion? Clearly impossible. I considered going to the doctor and I considered calling the police. I awoke the next morning atop a mountain of empty cans and bottles in the middle of the living room floor. I listened to the message again. A hundred times that night I had decided not to go to Doc

Holliday's and a hundred times I reversed that decision. At one point I'd made up my mind to bring a gun, but then thought better of it. On Saturday morning I took a shower and stood before the bathroom mirror as if preparing for a first date or an execution. To go would be to avoid insanity.

On the subway en route to the meeting I sat in the last car, averting my eyes from strangers and picking at the corner of a campaign sticker someone had placed on the window. As the train barreled through the tunnels I vacillated between love and hate, between fear and aggression. I envisioned twins, separated at birth, meeting thirty years later with an awkward handshake before the popping lights of news cameras, and then crumbling into one another's arms. I wondered if the other passengers on the train suspected me of criminal activity. Did I look dark? Perverted? I tried to remember the old westerns. What were the rules of a duel? Ten paces, turn and fire. I imagined choking him, killing him. I imagined kissing him on the mouth.

FIRST DRINK

He returns to the booth with a scotch in his hand. He lights a cigarette, shaking off my disapproving look. I sip my beer and we stare at each other. I am not the one who called this little meeting and I resolve not to be the one to break the silence. But he seems too aware of my resistance, and after awhile it feels petty, so I oblige him.

"We don't drink the hard stuff on Sundays," I scold him, "and we only smoke at night." I say this as casually as possible, so as not to come off a nag.

Oddly, I find myself eager to make a good first impression.

He takes a long drag off his cigarette and rests it in the glass ashtray between us. With a light-speed flash of his hand he removes the aviator glasses, and slides them into the breast pocket of his tuxedo coat.

My polar opinion of my own looks has always been a source of apprehension. Some days I consider myself repugnant; bug-eyed, sharp-nosed, short and pot-bellied, and will avoid social interaction in order to save embarrassment. Other days I find myself exceedingly attractive, far better looking than anyone on TV. But I have never, not once, not even for a second looked into a mirror and thought myself an average-looking man.

Looking across the table now my eyes are bluer than I imagined possible, and my face holds them out like jewels that could be concealed in an instant if shown aggression and then never be seen again. The bones of my head form a serious shape, and I look like a man who never tells jokes. The way I hold my posture is also striking; my shoulders high and my head leaning forward, tilting a bit to the side as if trying to find the proper angle to slip inside some brief opening. But most shocking are my deeply black pupils. They swim with intensity and seem to change temperature with every shifting glance. My stare is confident, self-satisfied. I look like a man always on the edge of smiling, but who would never quite cross that line.

And by the other's critical gaze I can guess how

I look to him right now—tired around the eyes, ashen, on the verge of illness. My whole body seems to beg forgiveness, except my chin, weak as it is, which somehow maintains some stoic defiance. My eyes dart about. My arms strain to lift the beer glass to my lips and when they finally do, my mouth parts awkwardly to accept the drink. I am so aware of every movement that my face cannot decide on an expression. Every visage seems awkward and wildly inappropriate, like those of an uncool teenager at his first school dance. And though all of my gestures can be inferred as timid, there is also a hint of intuition. Clearly my body language suggests passiveness, even frailty, but not without wisdom.

"First of all," he says, "I know what you're thinking, but you have to realize this is a rare opportunity and you shouldn't waste your time questioning this meeting. Obviously, there is a lot we could talk about. You can wonder all you want at the cosmic nature of this. You can sit there in disbelief and make me justify my being here. You can act like a man on trial. Before you even open your mouth, I want you to think about the good that can come of this. We have the same goal, right? We have not always agreed on how to achieve it. Today, we can come to some agreement. I urge you to take advantage of this. I know it's not your nature. Try and resist. You," he pauses, adjusting the already perfect bow tie of his costume. "We, I mean, are at a crossroads. Let's make some decisions here today, some policies that will serve as a code going forward so there can be less indecisiveness, less uncertainty. Do you know how much time we waste second-guessing our self? I think that today we have the chance to walk away from here a different person—clearer thinking, more balanced, well rounded. You think that perhaps I am your worst enemy. To the contrary, I am your only friend. Don't you think it's time we spoke? I want you to take a second and forget about the oddness of this encounter—it wouldn't hurt to have a stiffer drink—and just go with it, because not everyone gets this chance, and if there's one person who can make something come of it, it's us. It's you. What do you think?"

A long time passes before I return comment. "I admit to being stunned."

"Do you think you're dreaming?" he asks.

"I think that you are dreaming, and I am having a nightmare."

"If you think you are my idea of a dream," he says cleanly, "you might try and get to know me better."

"And if your idea of well-dressed is a prom outfit, you should have called a more congenial gal."

He gives me a deeper stare and I act as if it's not effective. Though his wardrobe calls for laughter, he wears it well. Tuxedos plead so strongly for attention. On him it works for one reason: he seems unaware he has it on.

"Our drinks are gone," he says.

SECOND DRINK

I sit with a full beer before me and he another scotch. He lights a cigarette and offers me one in a friendly way, politely accepting my refusal.

"If you're here to tell me something then go

ahead and say it." I still do not fully believe in him, but here he is in the flesh.

"I'm not here to tell you anything. I am here to talk. To each of our credit, we have become very adept in our positions. Unfortunately, our standoff has given way to gridlock. Inertia. Now I called this meeting because I knew you never would have—"

"My God," I blurt out.

"What?"

"I just never knew what an asshole I could be."

A grin comes across his face and he slaps the table hard. Then he breaks out into laughter and for the first time I recognize true warmth in him.

"There it is! You've seen yourself! Isn't it good? That's only fifteen minutes of your time, plus subway, and you've already learned something." He takes a dragon's drag of his cigarette and I think our booth will start afire.

I take a large swallow of beer and lean in.

"What exactly is it that we need to talk about?"

"I want to cure us of our chronic agnosticism."

"My what?"

"The constant indecision. It's mental masturbation!"

"Well, if you've got all the answers, fill me up: God or no God? To be or not to be? And don't leave out the career decisions."

"Listen," he says, holding up his finger authoritatively. "Very important. Don't do that. Accept one thing: I am not your fortuneteller. This is not *Highway to Heaven*. You can't come in here and talk to me like that."

"Talk to you like what?"

"Don't ask me to make decisions for you, because

you know what? We do not agree on anything. If we start in on that we'll be here all day and never get anything done."

He takes a thoughtful sip of his drink. "There's just no pressure out there," he says, motioning to the front door of the bar, "to decide. You see? Not these days. So I brought you in here."

His right index finger darts to his left shirtsleeve and he peels back his cuff, revealing the pearl-white face of the Citizen Quartz watch that was given to me by the Dean at my college. I seldom wear it on account of its formal nature. As a reflex, I look at my own wrist to see if I also have it on, and of course do not. I sense tension in him and with it surges that strange centrifugal force. A gust of gravity pushes against my face and body.

He thinks for a moment about what his watch is telling him and then finishes his drink.

"We can at least get a general understanding of each other. See the other side. I'm not just talking about you but me, too. We can achieve some kind of sharing. Like a trade-off."

"A balance of power."

"Absolutely not! Too much balance is the problem."

I finish the remainder of my drink in a drawn-out chug, knowing such adolesence will incense him.

"So you want to take turns making choices?" I inquire.

"Sounds a hell of a lot better than not making any."

"But it's good to be careful when making important decisions."

"It's good to be decisive when making them."
"It's best to be right."
"Exactly."

THIRD DRINK

    I grew up in Ohio except for the two junior high years we transferred to Washington so my dad could test ash after the eruption of Mt. St. Helens. In grade school in the suburbs we talked about drugs but never saw them. Instead we had this trick in which one kid stood behind another, wrapped his arms around the other's chest making a two-handed fist and applied all the pressure he could muster on the sternum of his friend, who held his breath and thirty seconds later fainted. When you went down you blacked out and did not remember it happening. While sleeping, which went on for up to five minutes, you had spectacular hallucinatory dreams and when you woke you felt sick and needed water. And though you could not remember having fainted, you always remembered the dreams. I only did this with my friend Abe McGlone, but we did it many times. Only once did I dream of a self-encounter.

    We were in his parents' basement. He had an older sister that I often pictured naked and she was there goading us to press harder, hold our breath longer, sleep deeper. *Twenty-seven, twenty-eight, twenty-nine.* When I went out, she was smiling over me, and as I faded away she dissolved in my vision with admiration in her eyes. I had done it for her. I slept for fifteen minutes—a neighborhood record. Halfway through my blackout, I hallucinated coming out of the bathroom and seeing myself lying on the floor. My body looked lifeless and the room was without sound. Abe's sister sat brushing back my hair as I slept, and in the corner of my vision I saw Abe sitting in a beanbag chair, red-faced, eyes intense as he played a hand-held video game.

"I just went to the bathroom," I said, but there were no words. "I'm glad I could do it even though I'm asleep over here." Abe and his sister ignored me so I yelled and heard a far away scream. And then, jealous of myself, I watched as Abe's sister leaned over to kiss my pale forehead.

I awoke in a damp spot on the floor with a pulsating headache and she was nowhere to be seen. But Abe, as my hallucination had promised, sat playing a video game in the beanbag chair.

For days I was haunted. Not from the image of my lifeless body but because in that instant all my prejudice had been swept away and I saw myself with clarity. The kid sprawled out there was some other kid, and I saw him exactly how I'd always seen strangers, with disturbing objectivity.

Now we are playing quarters and it seems that we are evenly matched. He is better at making the shot, but I am drinking beer to his scotch.

"Sometimes when a Top 40 song comes on we'll say screw it and just let it play. That's me," he declares.

He sips his new scotch. "If it were up to you all the time it'd be Crosby, Stills, Nash and Young morning, noon, and night. You make a provocative argument against the pitfalls of meaningless pop music but whatever, it's nice to drive to. Now Sinatra? There's something we both like, albeit for different reasons. And that's what I'm talking about. Trade-offs."

"I see. So you're Mr. Guilty Pleasure. I always wondered why I had those lapses in taste."

"Don't be so quick to judge." He tries to drink but begins laughing and has to set his glass down. "Now, who did that sound like?"

"I'll give you anything you want if you'll quit with the hair gel," I tell him.

"No more hair gel if you'll stop losing sleep over the origin of species."

We laugh drunkenly for a while and when we stop it takes a moment to remember what we were getting at, and who was who. At last I make a shot and he takes a drink without being told.

FOURTH DRINK

He offers me a cigarette and this time I accept. He lights it for me saying, "You see?" meaning that my smoking today had been in the cards and that I should not have resisted to begin with.

"We should use it more often, that's all I'm saying. Aren't we paying for it? You got to get out. I mean, we are paying for it anyway."

He is going on about how I need to use my car more frequently. How parking in the city is expensive and it only pays if we use the car.

"The car is a privilege," I tell him, but then realize I sound argumentative and add, "Well. It's a time thing. Weekends are precious."

"Yes. Every second is. That's why complacency is on the Most Wanted List."

"Come on, it's not like that. I didn't get from Ohio to Soho by staring at my navel."

"You also didn't get there alone. Who knows what things would look like today, had there been more direction? It hasn't exactly been a succession of informed decisions. Look at college. Look at our resume'. 1992? Perot. 1996? Perot. I wouldn't say we're exactly a hardliner." He points at his eyes with his index fingers. "It's not always crystal clear."

"Like it should be?"

The smoke from our cigarettes is not dissipating. It hovers at eye-level providing a sort of ceiling. He remains elegant in his tuxedo but his face, still striking, shows the effects of our discussion. A familiarity has settled in his expression, relaxing his stare, removing the rigidness in his posture. I feel a change in myself as well, less strained by nerves, my thought process more concrete. The force has declined so that now the contractions are fewer and further between and our bodies have synchronized a slow rhythmic motion, the equivalent to rocking back and forth in a cradle.

I smoke my cigarette down to the butt in silence before speaking.

"You and I, we have these arguments. Sometimes you win, sometimes I win. But we never know who's right. We never will. And I believe that—a person never knows where the other road would have led."

"Yes, but take this Tuesday for example. Now here's a chance to make a nice, clean choice."

"Tuesday?"

He puts his hand on mine for a brief second and the force swells up. My heart hurts and we both recoil in pain, but for a split second we are complete again.

He finishes his drink. "Now we're rolling," he says, and snaps his fingers.

He is a different kind of drunk than me.

FIFTH DRINK

He is muttering about a lack of direction, what he calls a culture of indecision. "Do you know what this is?" he asks. "People don't have to say yes or no anymore. They don't have to say red or blue. They just use the deferential passkey to every question ever asked and it makes them contemplative, objective. You know what it is." He has unhooked his bowtie. It hangs now on his neck like a collar.

"I don't know, tell me."

"That's it!"

We are at the jukebox, taking turns picking songs. Every time I punch in my selection he let's out a nasal sigh of disapproval.

I stop at the bar on the way back to our booth and order two scotches from the bartender.

"Maybe your brother needs a water," suggests the bartender.

"He's fine."

"You know, I had a buddy got left at the altar."

"Then you understand," I tell him. He says this round's on him.

When I return to the booth he's doing the thing with the invisible crumbs again.

"Another thing—I see you're finally having a real drink—no more of this guilt. From now on, missteps are forgotten. Dwelling on things is worthless."

"Sounds good to me."

"And then this other stuff, this middle-of-the-road deer-in-the-headlights issue. You just got to try it my way and—"

"I'm not sure I agree with your diagnosis. I mean, I do agree. I just don't think it's uniquely personal. You just said yourself. You just made it out to some kind of epidemic."

"True. But most people—let me tell you—most people, at least on the little things, feel one way or another. They don't wake up in the morning thinking their beer tastes great and go to bed thinking it's less filling. They have thoughts, beliefs, ideologies that are not in a constant state of flux. Most people don't challenge their positions on a daily basis."

"Most people are assholes."

"But look! We're up, we're down. We love everything, we hate it all. We swing back and forth between extremes on everything from God to the color of socks to wear. Global warming, Elian Gonzales, school vouchers."

"Free Mumia."

"—or let him hang. It's always you on one side, me on the other. It goes nowhere. And lately, with the first Tuesday of November fast approaching, it's becoming excruciatingly more acute. And yes, it's widespread, but we take it to a whole new level. This generation has a headache, but you've got a migraine."

Frazzled now, he leans back in his seat and sucks his cigarette. A bit undone, he still looks sharp in the way the Best Man looks sharp in the wee hours of the wedding—still heroic, but human now. I try to counter again, suggesting that he is perhaps mistaking apathy for impassioned disagreement, but it comes off clumsy and he either does not hear it or chooses to ignore me.

I want to be you, I think to myself.

"And I you," he says.

He is my darker half, the Alpha qualities, the physical strength. He is the risk-taker and the fighter and every one-night stand I've ever had. If wronged he would never forgive. Likewise he would never care to ask forgiveness. He is the math. He is the man you playfully slight before a group early on at a cocktail party, and later, at the door, deals you a far more public and memorable blow and then stares into your eyes as if to say, "Remember me?" Opportunism is his passion. He is also the responsible one, the one who keeps alphabetical files in a home office cabinet and remembers the dates on which things need to be done. He is the part of me who earns friendships, but not the part who maintains them.

I am the negotiator, the diplomat, the man who says the prayers at night. With a shrug and a smile, I see beyond the day and take comfort in perspective, offer it to others. I am the one with big dreams and a false sense of time, always thinking next week will bring change. I am also the haunted one, whose imagination can create psychological prisons. Two years ago I left a girlfriend suddenly, not because she'd done anything wrong but simply because she had the capacity to do wrong. This side of me allows such actions, allows the imaginary to count as reality. There are those who live in a world of theory and those who live in a world of practice. This side of me practices theory. This side of me is uneasy with things unseen, where as the other creature, he is content so long as the problem isn't stretched out in the road before him, begging for confrontation. But me, I am a seeker of problems, trying to right all the wrongs before time runs out.

SIXTH DRINK

Evening approaches, and the bar fills up. We stand together in semi-darkness outside the men's room, a few safe feet apart so as not to challenge the force.

"Let me tell you a story," I say. "You remember the obsessive Bart Larsen, that hockey player from freshman year. Here's a guy with opinions. Bumper stickers and t-shirts advertising his narrow mind. He had that out-of-state girlfriend, high school sweetheart. Pictures on his dorm room door. Remember? She cut him loose one month into his first year away at college. Naturally. Said she was still in high school, needed to grow at her own pace. Naturally. It's the same old story. Remember that kid? Could have had plenty of girls if he hadn't been so angry. Said he didn't love her and proved it a hundred times. So she cuts him loose and what does he do? Throws in the towel after first semester. Moves home to play semi-pro on that hack team her father coached. Tosses away a full scholarship. Now the one redeeming thing about this kid is that he got his ass out of South Dakota to get an education and play big time hockey. That's the only thing she could have liked about him. Was there anything else to like about Bart Larsen? His yellowed cotton briefs? I don't think so. So now that he throws that away, she's got zero reasons to like him. Even he knows that. So why'd he do it? Here's why: because he figures every time he scores a goal, every time he does something out there, he figures his goddamned coach—her goddamned father—is going to come home and mention his name over the family dinner while she sits there picking at her beef stroganov. Impact. That's what Bart wanted in the afterlife. He wanted to affect someone. To make it hard for her to forget him. Ever read about him in the sports page? No. No you did not."

"I liked Bart. Bart was a good guy."

"He wanted to leave a mark on everything he ever touched. That's the result of strong opinions."

He sits down on a bench at the end of the hall below an antique mirror framed in a giant horseshoe. I hear the toilet flush. He tightens his bow tie.

"The alcohol is your advantage," he says. "You're the philosopher, I suppose. I should have had you meet me for coffee."

"It'll be better this way," I tell him. "Balance is good."

The bathroom door opens and one of the bikers exits. I step inside the darkened room and search the tile wall for the light switch. Before I can find it I hear a hard breath. Two arms close around my chest, the hands forming a perfect fist at my sternum. My clawing fingers draw blood, draw blood, but fail. Instinctively I take a deep breath, close my eyes, begin counting to thirty...

SEVENTH DRINK

    The blue light of my television casts uneven shadows around the apartment as I stand before it undressing. I've got it on mute, making the C-SPAN anchor's facial gestures comical and absurd. He lowers his head, raises his eyebrows, looking now sincere, now provocative, now gentle. I hang my coat on a wire hanger and stuff my bow tie in the breast pocket. I sit on the couch in my boxers and pick up my drink from the floor. The ice cubes are the only sound in the room.

    This is the perfect program to watch with no sound. There are no highlight clips from basketball games, no cuts to ragged men in green running through the streets of Jerusalem. There is only this well-dressed man speaking with his eyes and his chin. Now he smiles carefully, so carefully that it is difficult to tell whether the news is good.

SQUALL
by Kristina Neihouse

Kristina Neihouse

Kristina Neihouse graduated from the University of Southern Maine in 1991 with a BA in English. Four years later she left the Maine winters behind, and moved to Key West with her husband, Andy Kimball. In 1996 they bought and moved aboard a 32' sailing Catamaran with their cats, Arlo and Hobo.

Kristina's had articles published in *Living Aboard* and *Multihulls Magazine*. Her full time work week is made up by a gift gallery on Duval Street, a new/used/rare bookstore, and shelving books at the county library. After six years Kristina and Andy made the decision to stay in P a r a d i s e .

In 2001, her story, "Squall", won the Key West Writing Contest in Fiction and will appear in *Key West: A Collection*.

Squall

I had been at the library reading magazines between my morning and evening jobs. When I left the parking lot on my bicycle, the rain drops were few but fat. I made it one block before it started to pour. I pulled under the awning of the Marquesa Cafe, put the kickstand down on my bike and sat on the brick step to wait. A man crossed Simonton Street on his bicycle and pulled under the awning. He propped his bike against the pole and sat next to me. We smiled at each other.

"Another day in Paradise," he said.

I recognized him. He worked at the Faustos Deli. I bought black bean salad or tabouli from him. We usually exchanged small talk about the weather and the tourists. He had on cut-offs and a faded T-shirt. His baseball cap was spotted with rain.

"Day off?" I asked.

"My one day weekend."

"I know about those," I said.

"What the tourists don't want to hear when they ask what it's like to live in Paradise."

A man and woman ran down the sidewalk. He had a fanny pack belted around his waist. She had a large hat tied on with a flowered scarf. They were carrying their sandals and running through the puddles. I watched until I could no longer hear their laughter and shrieks.

"I do think of leaving sometimes," I said. "But that's as far as I get."

"Just can't get motivated enough for the rest," he said, finishing my thought. "It's certainly no vacation to live here, but it's a hard place to leave."

"I had never been here before," I told him. "I used to live in New England. I woke up one morning and just knew I couldn't handle another winter. A month later I packed my car and headed south until I ran out of road."

"Sold your car?" He asked.

"I needed the money to rent a house."

He laughed.

"You too?"

"I rent a house I share with four other people."

"I have three roommates," I said. "Paradise isn't cheap."

"It sure isn't."

I looked at the street. This wasn't the usual quick downpour followed by clear steamy skies. It was still raining hard and the sky was gray as far as I could see over the La Concha hotel one block away. I looked at him. He was already looking at me. His eyes were light blue, almost gray but brighter than the sky. He bent to retie the lace of his sneaker.

"It can be lonely," I said, looking back at the street.

"What?" He looked back at me. I bent to scratch my shin.

"Can't it be lonely?"

"Definitely," he said. "It's easy to meet people but hard to get to know them. Everyone works so much. It seems people are always leaving, changing jobs or moving. It's hard to keep track."

"Businesses too." I said. "As soon as I find a place to have coffee or get lunch between jobs, the place is sold or they just close down. I've almost given up."

He nodded. "My main hangout is my front porch."

The wind picked up and blew rain in where he sat. He moved over. We were now sitting very close. The pavement was wet all around us.

"But," I said. "The weather doesn't suck."

"Usually," he said.

A woman rode by on a bicycle. She was trying to hold a newspaper over the small dog in her basket. The sky was still gray with rain and I was late for work. I didn't care.

"There are things that I love," I said. I could see him looking at me out of the corner of my eye. I focused on my fingernails.

"I like to check the sky every night, see where the moon is, or how many stars are out. I rode down to Higgs beach once when the power went out. The moon was full. It was so bright, there were shadows. I had never seen a moonshadow before."

"I went out on my porch when that happened. I could read the headlines in the newspaper by the light of the full moon."

"That's all I read anyway," I said.

"Me too," he laughed.

There was a cat sitting on the step of the antique shop across the street. I watched it cleaning its face.

"How about when you do see someone who changed jobs or moved," I said. "If you run into them at Winn Dixie or the post office. It's such a surprise. It almost feels like we're all in an exclusive club, that we share this special place."

I looked at him. His eyes were brighter than the gray light of a full moon.

"It is special," he said.

"Maybe that's why we don't leave."

"I'm not ready," he said.

"For what?"

"To be a part of it all again."

I stretched my leg. My sandal was now touching

his sneaker. I didn't know what to say, but I knew what he meant. He looked at me.

"You know," he said. "There is an isolation down here. A comfort at being so far away."

"I don't think people take this place seriously," I said. "They come down to go snorkeling, get drunk, buy a T-shirt and go home."

"Good riddance," he said, still looking at me. "We're still here."

He didn't say anything for a few minutes. The rain was steady but not as loud.

"It's easy here," he said, "to blame work and the cost of living for not having the time to do anything or even care."

"Sometimes it's easier that way."

"Sometimes," he said.

The street drain was clogged. A car drove by and washed water onto the sidewalk. It almost reached our bicycles. I turned to him. His forehead was wrinkled in concentration. He seemed to be studying my face. I wondered if he could see the small pimple on the side of my nose. I wondered if he would care. He was so close.

Another car splashed by and then we were kissing. We moved and turned at the same time so that our noses didn't bump, and our lips met softly. I closed my eyes in the silence, and wondered how this had happened. His lips were dry on the outside but smooth and warm where they met mine. I wanted to reach for his hand, to feel for calluses or the soft skin of his palm.

Then I noticed the silence. He must have noticed as well. We stopped kissing and looked at the street. The rain had stopped. I could still see dark clouds but they were moving away. There were weak shadows on the sidewalk.

"It stopped," I said. I could see him nod out of the corner of my eye. I looked at my watch but did not notice the time. "I have to get to work."

"I'll be making fresh tabouli tomorrow," he said.

"Great, I'll stop by." I looked at his hand resting on his knee. I still wanted to know how it felt.

"I'll see you tomorrow," he said.

"Tomorrow."

I got on my bike and rode away trying to avoid the puddles.

THE GUIDE TO SAFE CAMPING

Camping Tip #1

The Two Types Of Camping
as Defined by the Required Supplies

Type I - Hiking Camping

<u>Gear</u>
Therma-Rest
Frisbee (acts as a plate as well)
Fleece
Rope
Flashlight
Collapsible fishing pole
Sleeping bag
Tent
Toilet paper

<u>Food</u>
English Muffins
Peanut Butter
Jelly (Blueberry?)
Ramen Noodles (avoid the shrimp, use 1/2 seasoning)

<u>Drink</u>
Water
Whiskey

Type II - Car Camping

<u>Gear</u>
Paper Plates
Fleece
Flashlight
Sleeping bag
Tent

<u>Food</u>
Hot Dogs
Mustard/Ketchup
Marshmallows
Graham Crackers
Chocolate
Ramen Noodles (avoid the shrimp, use 1/2 seasoning)

<u>Drink</u>
Water
Beer
12-pack of Mountain Dew

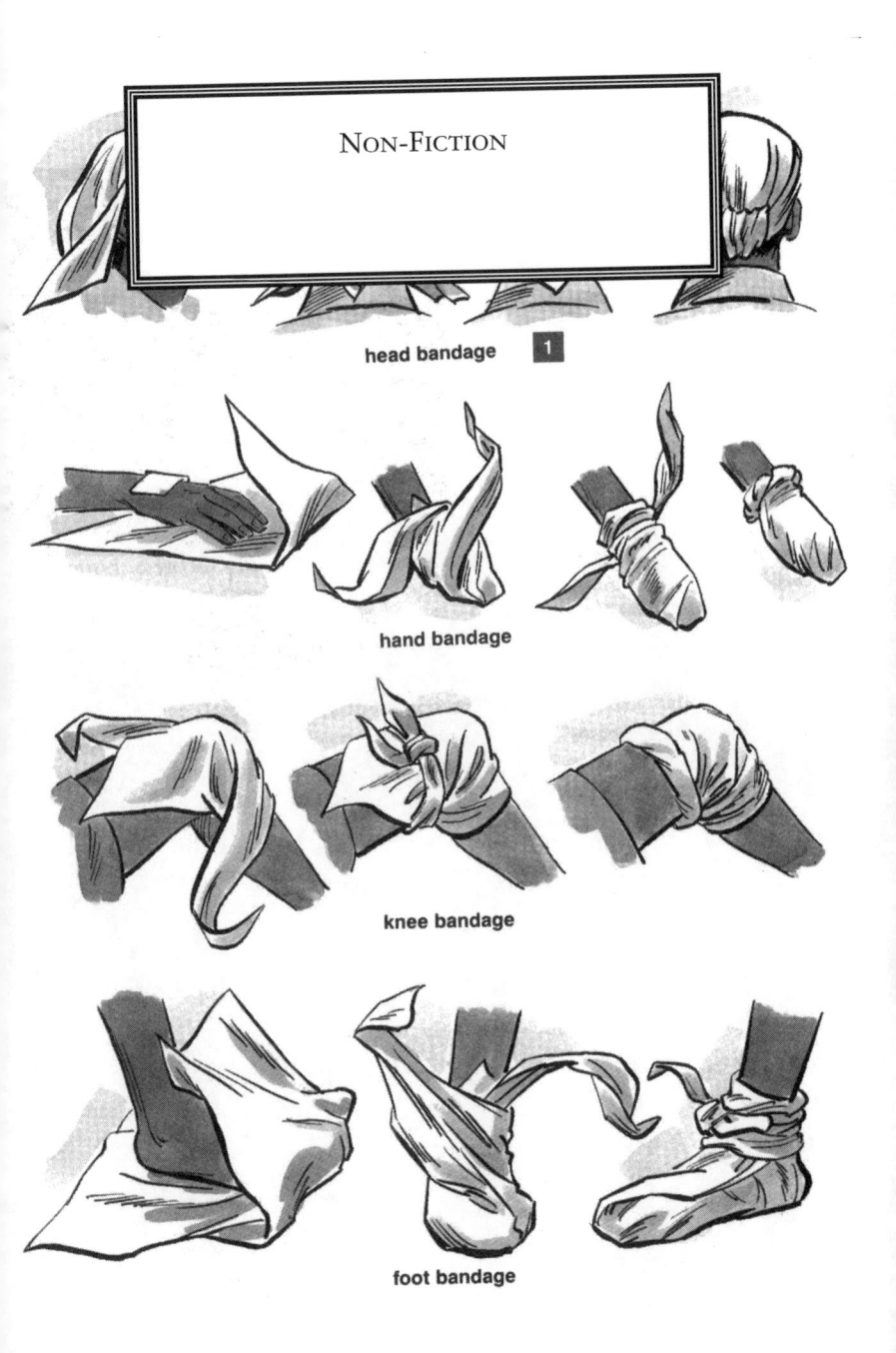

Non-Fiction

head bandage 1

hand bandage

knee bandage

foot bandage

Key West: The Peaceable Kingdom
By
Linda Fasano List

Linda Fasano List

Linda grew up in Northern New York State near the St Lawrence River and attended Long Island University in Brooklyn.

In 1980 she moved to Colorado where she and her husband own a candy factory and produce hand made candy. Their candy has been featured in many publications such as *Martha Stewart Living*, *Gourmet*, and *Sunset Magazine*.

She and her husband lived in Key West for two years, 1995-1997, and operated a tropical candy store on Duval Street. Linda is a member of the Key West Women Writers Collective.

In 2001, "Key West; The Peaceable Kingdom" won the Key West Writing Contest in Non-Fiction. Her winning piece will appear in *Key West: A Collection*, published by White Fish Press.

Key West: The Peaceable Kingdom

Key West is often called "The Last Resort" or "The End Of The Road", due to its status as the end of US Route 1 (or the beginning, depending on one's perspective). Locals call it "The Conch Republic", after seceding from the Union a few years back, during a dispute with the Federal Government over traffic stops to check for drugs. One tourism slogan welcomes visitors to "The Florida Keys, A State Of Mind". Charles Kuralt, in one of his travel books, refers to Key West as "America's Most Tolerant City" due to its "live and let live" atmosphere.

Personally, I like to think of Key West as "The Peaceable Kingdom". It's like the famous painting of all the different animals, normally together only as predator and prey, sitting together in peaceful co-existence. Key West is truly an experiment in humanity. All sorts of humanity, frequently in conflict in other parts of the world, peacefully co-exist on one island about two by four miles wide.

A recipe for Key West might read like this:

Start with some writers, poets, artists, and wannabes; mix in a large group of gays and lesbians; add some old salt "boaties"; some homeless runaways seeking warm sunshine; and a handful of street derelicts and crazies. Cuban descendants of old time cigar makers, and Bahamians descended from slaves and fisherman; create some extra spice; And don't forget a few do good Christians trying to dominate all the other powerful flavors; Fold in a few million tourists from all over the world; decorate freely with 80,000 cats and a few well-loved dogs. Amazingly the results can be quite pleasing.

Key West is a tourist town. It's a haven for Northerners seeking escape from the winter cold, a respite for misfits seeking relief from ordinary life, and a destination for tourists on a cruise ship or tour bus seeking a photo op at the Southernmost Point of the United States.

Festivals throughout the year attract partygoers interested in celebrating whatever is on the schedule. "Hemingway Days" is for Ernest Look-a-likes, Hemingway-philes, and would-be authors. "The Gay Arts Festival" celebrates everything creative produced by the Gay Community.

This is followed by "Mini Lobster Season" bringing amateur lobster catchers and connoisseurs of Florida Lobster (these crustaceans only have tails—no pinchers like their Northern cousins). Fall brings "Womanfest" when the lesbians of the world unite for a week, followed by the Harley-Davidson Poker Run, getting tamer every year as the Harley-loving Baby Boomers reach 50 and can't stay awake past midnight! (Bars here are open 'til 4 a.m. if you care to drink to the real wee hours of the morning.)

The most popular and famous celebration is Fantasy Fest, attracting 50,000 revelers to this small island. Fantasy Fest is an "adult" celebration. A decency panel would endow an "X" rating on the revelry.

A new theme each year, such as "Tinseltown Dreams" or "Call Of The Wild" provides the guidance for creative floats and costumes that are often planned a year in advance. Anything goes on Duval Street–drinking, partying, parading to show off costumes (or lack of!)–well, almost anything.

Air-brushed bare breasts, resembling flowers in full bloom, and a nude motor bike rider have been known to test the patience of local authorities. Gay Bars hold tea dances in the streets, and drag queens show off their sequined gowns and elaborate hairdos. Key West's beloved pets are included in the fun with the Annual Pet Parade. Owners dress their pets in elaborate costumes and perform skits and songs to show off their animals and compete for prizes.

In spite of all the craziness, Fantasy Fest benefits a serious charity, AIDS Help Inc. Hundreds of thousands of dollars have been raised over the years for this local favorite charity.

Key West is a caring community. When a block of historic Duval Street burned one summer, many employees were left without jobs. Benefits were immediately held to raise money to see employees through until they secured new jobs. Key West is a humanitarian community. Local grocery stores have donation boxes for food for homeless cats. Free and low cost spay and neuter clinics are held monthly to help contain the homeless animal population.

If you want a fancy obituary, Key West is a good place to end your days. I don't know who writes these final announcements, but I'd like to sign them up to write mine! A few samples read as follows:

"Ruth E. Parker, age 83 died Thursday. She was known as Key West's own Carol Channing. Ruth was an actress in Key West live stage for 27 years. She dabbled as an artist, and was an accomplished seamstress. Ruth smoked filterless camels for 60 years. Services were not requested."

"William Divens died suddenly at age 25. He was probably best known in Key West for his love and refurbishing of Volkswagens."

"Michael Stanley Barrett passed from this life on Tuesday morning. He was affectionately known as "Mike" by family and friends. Mike fought his illness with courage and dignity and lived his life by spiritual principles."

These tributes seem to embody the spirit of Key West', "Peace On Earth, Good Will To Men—all men and women regardless of race, religion, creed, or lifestyle—and animals, too!"

MIDNIGHT MIND NUMBER TWO

THE GUIDE TO SAFE CAMPING

Camping Tip #2

Camping Soundtrack

Car Camping is only as fun as the music. Below is required car camping music for you (and the families camping next to you) to enjoy.

1. Sweet Melissa - Allman Brothers Band
2. Tom Sawyer - Rush
3. The Wreck of the Edmund Fitzgerald - Gordon Lightfoot
4. Dream On - Aerosmith
5. Bad Company - Bad Company
6. Money - Pink Floyd
7. Jungle Love - Steve Miller band
8. Sweet Home Alabama - Lynyrd Skynyrd
9. Honky Tonk Woman - Rolling Stones
10. American Girl - Tom Petty and the Heartbreakers
11. Feel Like Makin' Love - Bad Company
12. Margaritaville - Jimmy Buffett
13. Casey Jones - Grateful dead
14. Country Roads - John Denver

Poetry

BUCKING A LOG

1

2

3

Mallory Square
By
Jeff Mann

Jeff Mann

Jeff Mann grew up in Covington, Virginia and Hilton, West Virginia. He received undergraduate degrees in English and forestry at West Virginia University in 1977 and an M.A. in English in 1984.

His poems and essays have appeared in many magazines, including *The Laurel Review*, *Callaloo*, *Journal of Appalachian Studies*, *Poet Lore*, and *Prairie Schooner*.

His first chapbook of poetry, *Bliss*, won the 1997 Stonewall Chapbook Competition. *Mountain Fireflies*, which won the 1999 Poetic Matrix Chapbook Series, and *Flint Shards from Sussex*, which won the 1999 Gival Press Chapbook Competition, were published in 2000.

He lives in West Virginia and Virginia, where he teaches creative writing and literature at Virginia Tech.

In 2001, his work, which won the Key West Writing Contest in Poetry, will appear in *Key West: A Collection*.

Mallory Square

Deathbed of aquamarine, bridal train of bronze—
we come to share the sun's theatric daily demise,

to watch trained cats leap through hoops,
clumsy acrobats chuck about on stilts.

Perfectly still, men painted white
pose as toga-draped statues,

as if that flesh deemed
most beautiful the gods might make

marble. A sunset-crowd of hundreds,
and here we all reach the end

of something: this blue-brine
extremity, this island edge.

Behind mangrove keys, to applause
the sun sinks off the Isle of Bones,

this erstwhile Indian graveyard become
rum-rich Eden. Long and lingering

the horizon billows
with crematory fire.

Where do we go from here?
Back to a yearning for more,

knowing more will not satisfy?
The crowd disperses in twilight

chill, the sea goes gray as ash.
On the dock-edge, you hold

my hand, we name
what constellations we can.

Of Bikes and Lovers

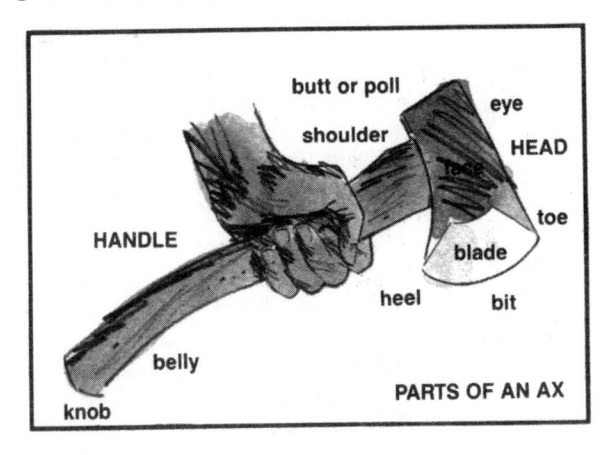

[Illustration: Parts of an ax — butt or poll, shoulder, eye, HEAD, face, toe, blade, heel, bit, HANDLE, belly, knob]

By
Cristina Perissinotto

Cristina Perissinotto

Cristina Perissinotto was born in Northern Italy. Her poetry has appeared in *Poetry Motel*, *The Lucid Stone*, and *White Pelikan Review*. She has published articles on Renaissance and contemporary literature in *La Nuova Venezia*, *Romance Languages Annual* and various anthologies. She lives in Italy and is working on a book of Renaissance travels.

Of Bikes and Lovers

He did not want anything too gaudy for her
but it ended up matching the flamingoes
on the lawn. A kid's bike almost,
that ran merrily on winding paths.

The waves would hit them like daylight
on dog days. They rose and fell,
rose and fell, luscious seaweed
carried by the tide. His skin
was an ocean of white paper
that shivered and rippled,
broke and sparkled. Every afternoon
yielded ripe oranges,
whose juices dripped down
her fingers, palms, wrists.

In the backyard the sausage tree
loomed low and mysterious
by the laundry shed.
She often saw the hand
of Disney in the landscape.

Life's scent was intense, in those days.
All they looked for, with hungry eyes,
trembling souls, was time alone,
a most precious gift. He and his wife
would grill sausages, and have her over
for a meal in the breezy kitchen.
She would look up at the cathedral
ceiling and fear divine retribution.

He loved her for two reasons only,
her skin, and her mind. But her skin
was too smooth, her mind too wanting.

In the tropical winter sun,
when life spread ahead like a string
of Venetian beads, they failed
to anticipate future thunders and regrets,
icy winters and separations.

So they rose and fell, rose
and fell, drinking from each other's
words like thirsty seagulls.
They had little dates in Formica diners.
He would enclose her knees in his
across the table and ask
how should we call our first daughter.
Anna, she would say, while the pink
waitress refilled their cups
and commented on the listless weather.

Do not wish upon the pregnant clouds
on the aqua line between sky and water,
as they are marks of deception.
At night, he wished her sweet dreams
before going to sleep in his own bed.

All night and all day she would long
for his lanky, loving legs.
Banana leaves curled around
their mixed happiness.
She refused to wake up,
as her dreams were fragrant of lavender
and fresh wishes. He and his wife
visited alligator-ridden swamps,
while she had a date every day at three
with the rain.

MIDNIGHT MIND NUMBER TWO

The morning of each day
they awoke to a new song
(while their nightmares remained
unraveled) and pedaled to work.
At the crossing, waiting for the light to turn,
he would stop, glance at the cars
passing by, smile widely and say so,
how about a kiss.

Fossil and Prints:
Two Poems

By

Christian
Langworthy

Christian Langworthy

At one time, Christian was actually a cool guy. He was an Army infantry officer during the time of the Gulf War. He'd spend his weekends in the back woods of Georgia on road marches carrying at least 100 lbs. of crap. It was then that he began to think about writing, because it required only light materials. So he left the Army and moved to Chicago to pursue writing and a woman nicknamed Holly Golightly. She was swell. Christian wrote whenever she wasn't around. Then one day he moved to Binghamton, home of Rod Serling and a lot of weird twilight people. Deep in that valley, Christian wrote poetry and his first attempts at fiction. It all sucked pretty much except for a few poems. Then one day, Christian moved to Manhattan to go to Columbia—not the country, but that strange place uptown. While there, he pursued a woman named Lynn who now lives in California. Right now, Christian lives in Greenpoint among the Polish community, giving them ethnic diversity with his Asiatic looks.

Fossil

So I was unearthed and they
Found hints of feathers on my bones.
I wish I could tell them I didn't fly
That I hung around waiting for
The inevitable weight of air.

Prints

The day was brisk and windy, the thunderheads
Rolled wet leaves over the city, leaves
Pressed onto the blackened streets like Japanese prints.
The fresh scent of new rain hangs in the air.
Thoughts of you come only like this—
Why does Autumn undress the way you do?

Yesterday, I thought of black umbrellas.
I had read one of Max Jacob's poems with
Black umbrellas in it a few weeks back,
So perhaps that was why, the bodies like mushroom stems—
Rigid, damp, and cold, coping with the heavy rain
As best they could, each tethered
To the wet-blackened streets.

Today the wet streets lay smudged with the colors
Of passing cars and buses
And shining headlights.
The way you are in my head is like a painting
Speaking to a stranger years later.
The city hums with life, a city of elevated
Trains, wires, and fire escapes waiting
For someone's misfortune.
Brown, wet leaves lay flattened
Against the black streets. I think of the Japanese
Prints we saw together at the Institute
And of a haiku by Basho.

MIDNIGHT MIND NUMBER TWO

Three Michigan Poems
By
Marie Bahlke

Marie Bahlke

"I'm a native of Duluth, Minnesota and have been playing with words since I was very young. In recent years I have become increasingly serious about poetry, and now at 81 find it my way of looking at, thinking about, and dealing with my long life."

Memory

A mystery of small parts –
the deck spread
face-down between us.
Cross-legged she sat
on the floor
blonde hair
obscuring her smile
as she flipped
pairs of twos
slapped queen to queen
ten to ten
till our square was
pocked and her
pairs piled up.
Uncanny, the see-
through glasses of
her mind.

Now the knaves turn up
singly
faces aslant
proffering tarts.
And she plays
a loaded deck.

Going to Mendon in October

Osage orange trees border the road
their fruit green in a season of dying.
We talk of this when we reach the house
by the river
where it's a bad day for Mary.
We've walked at the Mill and
bring her leaves—yellows and reds,
winey maroons.
She lets them fall on her quilt
as we speak of the river,
leaf patterns in the current,
her sense of peace living on a river,
moving water her mantra.

We'd been neighbors long before,
our back doors eye to eye.
Dubbing ourselves the Happiness Club,
we grieved for daughters, lost
opportunities. Then ate her fennel cookies
and talked of books, as narcotic to her as gin.
Talent leapt from her fingers—the sound
of her piano through my kitchen window.

In time they wandered, then weary
settled at the river's edge. Again we met,
our husbands sometime guests,
picnicked beside another stream,
she with her thermoses of warmth—
consommé and wine.
Restive, she wrote till her pages
stretched to novel length.
And then the siren call of books:
the town made her librarian.
She swept the shelves
paired Alcott with Baraka.

And now this bitter challenge.
Through seven stages till
acceptance came,
her anger shook this house.
Today in her quiet bed
Tongue loosened by the
lateness of the hour
she lets her secrets fall.
Then grieving done
she comforts me.

I wear her ring
its forthright stone
the color of her eyes.
Demanding action
It fits my index finger.

Pacifist

You once shot two birds
then laid down your gun,
done with killing
even in the press of war
until the ducks
were suddenly beneath our wheels.
As if you'd aimed and fired
small bodies burst with quiet force.
When you could, you stopped the car—
feathers, bits of flesh,
and that muted sound of killing
buried in our heads.

MIDNIGHT MIND NUMBER TWO

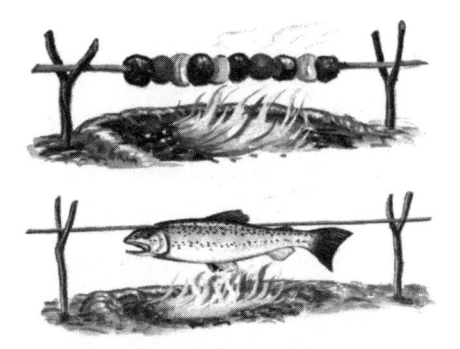

Tobacco Farmer's Wife
and Losing Faith
By
Marion Boyer
author of stories, poems, etc.

Marion Boyer

Boyer has had poetry printed most recently by *Atlanta Review*, *The Driftwood Review* and *Hurricane Alice*. In the fall edition of *Education Travel Review* her poems were selected as "best writing of the edition" by the editor.

Tobacco Farmer's Wife

It's Kentucky fall again, that gold color,
like looking through a glass of hard cider.
The tobacco's strung like wrinkled laundry
up to the big barn, full up to the rafters,
       three tiers drying out.
Garden's rotting away.
You scuff the dirt with that steel-toed boot,
slide your hands inside them pockets
so they don't come loose, I expect.
Staring off at nothing. Thinking maybe
winter's coming, like that big-horned steer
moves so heavy.
       What's this world coming to, old man,
now your mind's gone up in smoke?
Fifty-three years. Half the time
you don't know me. Hit me bad
enough in our own bed for stitches.
       Who'd you think I was?
They put you a night in jail like some criminal.
Look at you—going to the barn,
stripping them leaves, bundling them up
like pages of our days
folks'll just burn up to air.
       There ain't much left to do—
no more than an acre to strip and bundle.
We'll tie 'em up tight, old man
I'm fixing to help.

Losing Faith

When I was little I made a box
with a pinhole to capture
the sun in eclipse.
It was a dangerous time:
snow had nuclear fallout,
traffic could flatten a child
who didn't look both ways.
But, I held the sun in a box.
It was small like me.

Over our street, one night,
Sputnik passed
through the fastened stars,
moving mechanically, slow.
I traced it with my eyes
not knowing the dog inside
was already dead.
I was in love with infinity ~
Bigger than forever and ever, Amen.
Infinity.

I am nearing fifty.
Infinity seems a fairytale.
I traveled to the Grand Canyon,
became small again.
I came to learn geologic time,
while immense,
is finite.

I returned to the street of my childhood
and there it was as before,
the same trees, houses, and the sky above.
And yet, I can not see how to
box in the sun again.

MIDNIGHT MIND NUMBER TWO

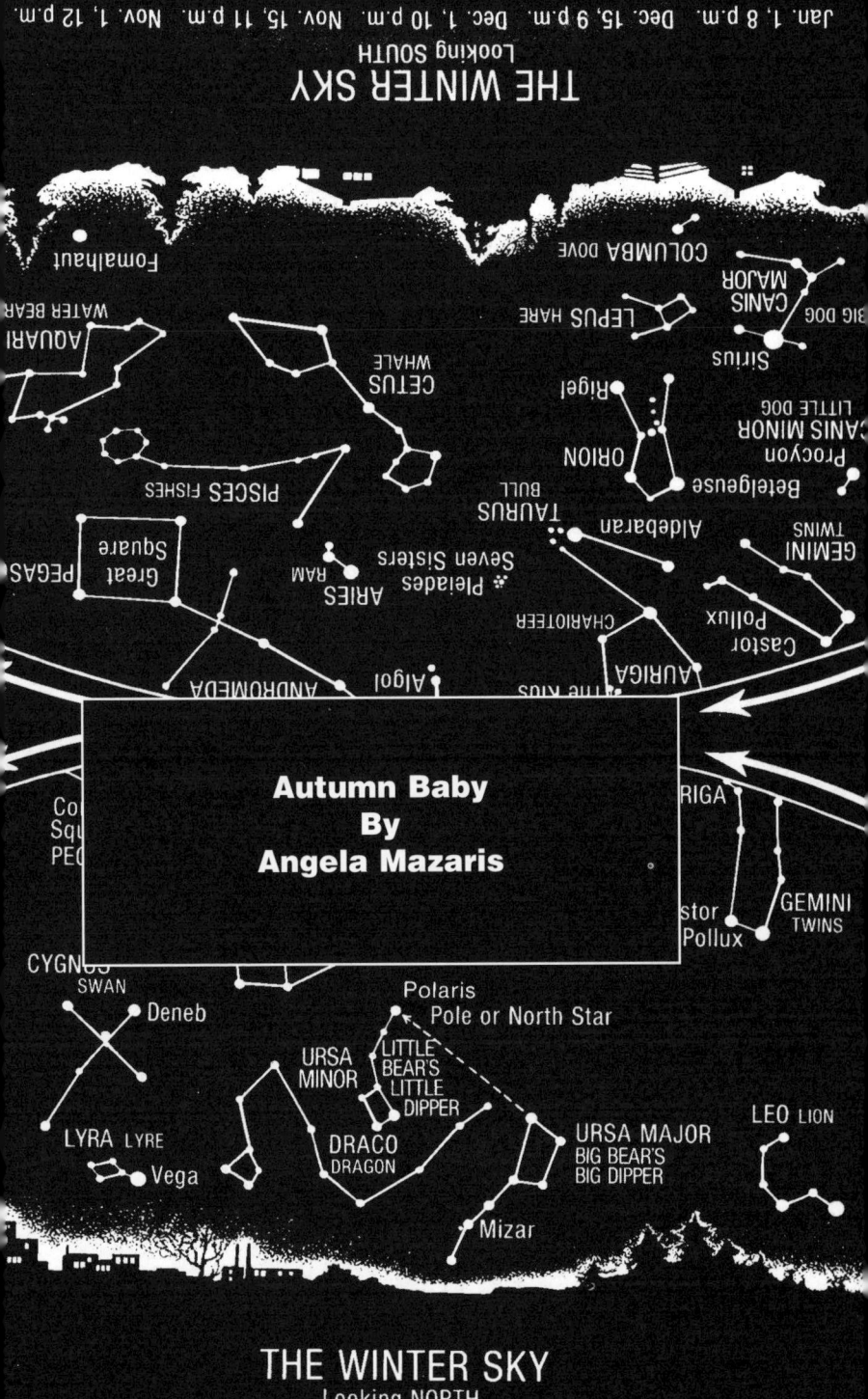

Autumn Baby
By Angela Mazaris

Angela Mazaris

Angela Mazaris is a writer and teacher, currently residing year-round on Nantucket. In 2001, her work appeared in *Nantucket: A Collection*, published by White Fish Press.

Autumn Baby

In these days that straddle summer and fall,
the light comes alternatively thick and thin.

I have always been an autumn baby,
grateful for the last rays of sun on skin,
and never forgetting that winter is on its way.

SEMAPHORE CODE

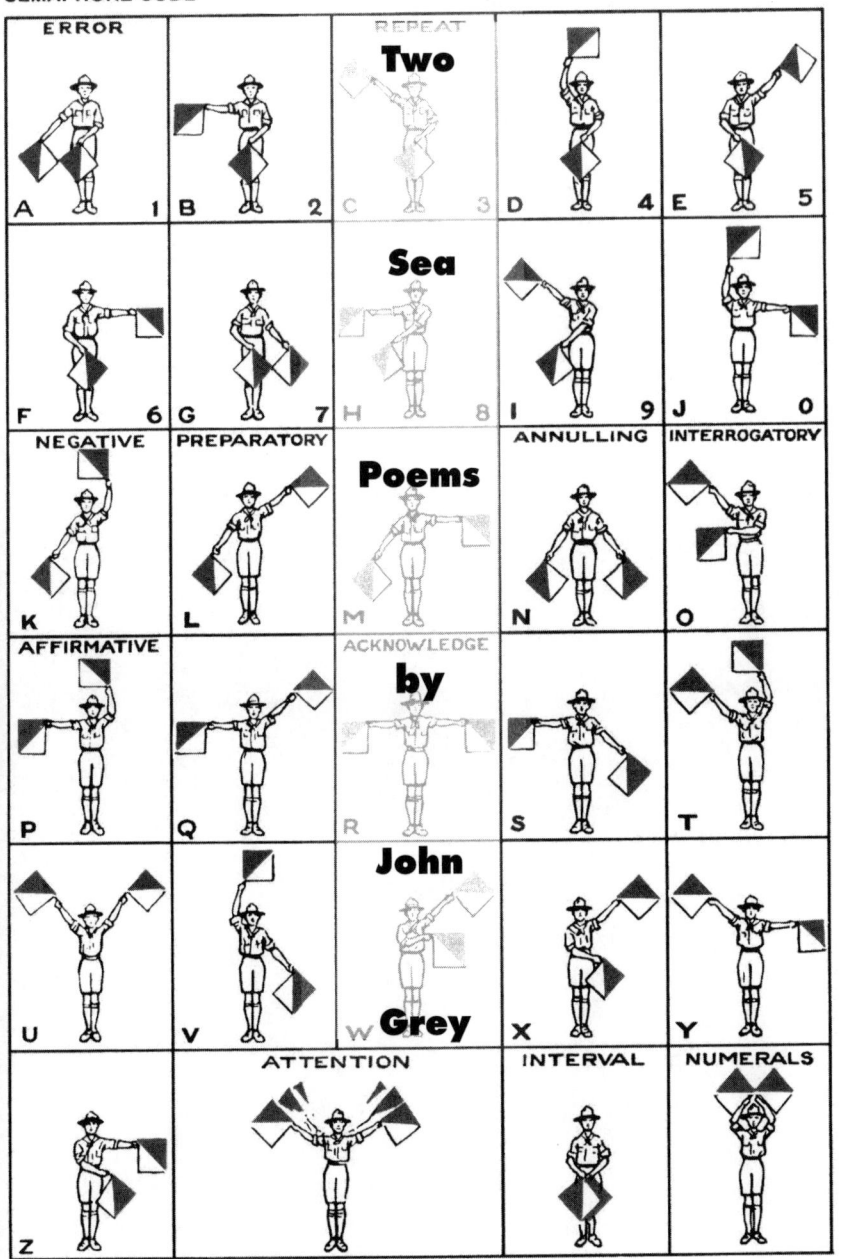

Two Sea Poems by John Grey

John Grey

John lives in Providence, Rhode Island. He has had work published in journals including *Bottomfish, Whetstone, South Carolina Review*, and many others.

In 2001, his work appeared in *Nantucket: A Collection*, published by White Fish Press.

Shipwreck in the Reef

Busted planks
jut out of the sand
like staghorn,
like pillar coral.
The wreck is long since
stripped of any treasure
but the reef still dazzles
more than Aztec gold,
than Spanish doubloons.
Still, I snorkel the decks
of this sunken boat,
peer in through its ghostly portholes.
All around me,
in pale blue rippling water,
I can hear the silence
of the men who sailed it.
It's like the warmth,
the relief, of meeting someone
in a foreign land
who speaks the same language.
A ray slips through the doorway
and I follow.
In a cabin of all voices,
currents spin the wheel.
An angelfish flutters
by my right shoulder
and toward the light
as it should.
An eel slithers
beneath me
and down into a swirling dark.

Sunset Celebration

Some juggle light,
some sell it with
their jewelry,
the last of the sun
glinting its laser beams
from necklace to eye.
Some strum it,
or drum it
like the gallop
of the horse.
Sunset makes noise,
bursts with red and yellow laughter.
From the rose-tipped ruffle
of the sea,
to the lingering haze
of the palm branches,
to the blossoming orange faces,
the bright edge of the world
is everywhere you look.

To a Poet, To the West
By
Louis S. Faber

Louis S. Faber

Louis S. Faber is a corporate attorney, student (MFA in Creative Writing) and poet living in Rochester, NY. He has been writing and publishing for many years, most recently appearing in the *Worcester Review, Borderlands, Midstream Magazine, Chaminade Literary Review, Blueline* and elsewhere. His poetry has also appeared in publications in Canada and England. He intends to keep writing until he gets it right.

To a Poet, To the West

Richard Wilbur lives in Massachusetts
and in Key West, Florida according
to his dust jackets. If you set sail westward
from San Diego you may find your dream
of China, of the endless wall which draws
the stares and wonder more foreboding
more forbidden even than the city,
which you visit to sate yourself of lights,
sirens and the blood heat of steam grates.
It is easier than digging and far less
dirty, and the walls of the sea rise
more slowly. Once it was a risky journey
the danger of the edge looming over the horizon,
but then digging was no option, pushing deeper
with your crude shovel, knees bloody,
until, at last, you broke through
with dreams of the dragon as you fell
into the limitless void. Now you sail
with dreams of the Pacific sky, although
water has no need of names. The poet
has grandchildren now, and it is to them
to dream of the China that was.

FLORIDA
A POEM BY SARAH BROWNING

Sarah Browning

Sarah Browning is the winner of the first annual Quadrangle Award. She has published poems in numerous journals such as *The New York Quarterly, The Literary Review, The Seattle Review, Mudfish,* and *Sycamore Review*. She was founding director of Amherst Writers & Artists Institute, an organization providing creative writing workshops to low-income women and youth, and now works raising money for The Fund for Women Artists. She was Visiting Artist at Northfield Mount Hermon School in the 1999-2000 school year.

Florida

My pinkly skin turns dark red
in the pinky-yellow sun. The great pink
hotel sells red and yellow and pink ice
blender drinks by the flowering
pink trees by the blue blue pool.
White ibis peck their long red
beaks to the white white sand
and I am pink and white and pink
again under my pressing thumb.

My chambermaid takes two buses
to the beach to change my white sheets
six days per week to feed
her four out of six black children
still breathing—two of them
still nursing. The first died when his momma
was 13 and another was a boy too
who died too which is why God
gave me all boys she said
and I named one of my babies
after one of the ones who passed
so I still think of the first Joseph
but I don't talk to the boys
about the ones I lost, but
I still think about them.

Only three green dollars in my purse.
Do I rush out to an ATM? Do I ask
my chambermaid's address? I know all manner
of manners but I don't know
which is tackier, to apologize
for not having more money
in my little black purse
or not to apologize, knowing
full well that I am rich
to her either way, that I'm older
than her too with just my one boy.
I give her my $3.
I don't apologize.
I go into the ocean and float.
The bright yellow sun
looks down on my white white
shoulders and burns them.

MIDNIGHT MIND NUMBER TWO

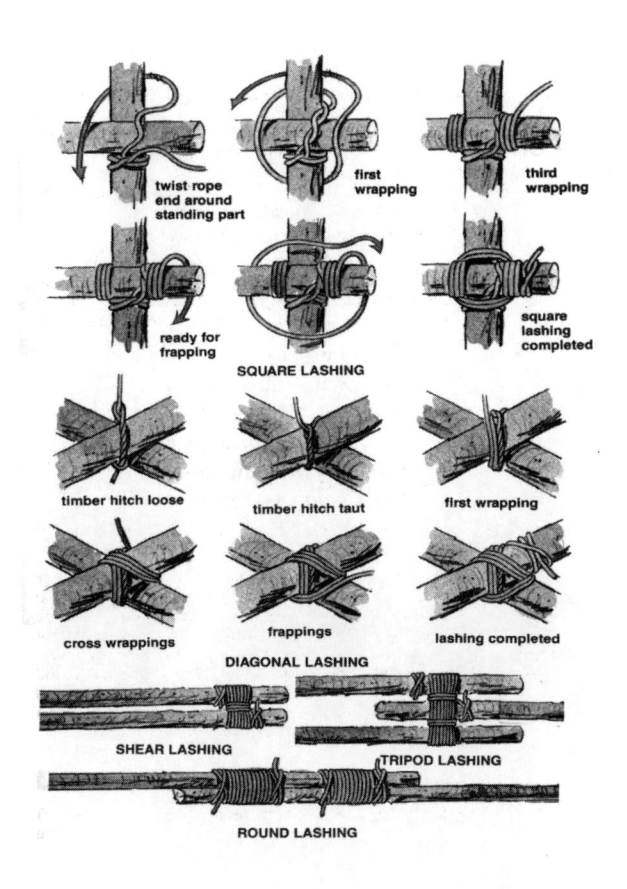

Unnecessary Junk

& *two other poems*

by
Dianalee Velie

Dianalee Velie

Dianalee Velie is a graduate of Sarah Lawrence College and she has a Master of Arts in Writing from Manhattanville College's MAW program, where she has taught the craft of writing. She has also taught at Norwalk Community College and at the State University of New York. Her summer island workshop, Belden Island Magic, continue to attract sold out sessions.

When I Leave Your House

I wake to the absence of your scent
displaced by the aroma of coffee
spiraling up the stairs.

I know I will find you composed
at the computer, lost
in impenetrable space,

your world of words,
widowed sweat pants, a blank
black T-shirt, cut off and frayed

around the neck, hair pulled
back from your face
where bifocals hide the lines

of concentration etching
into your existence,
silent stanzas of sorrow defined in flesh.

I know you will not get up
when I leave your house,
even as I kiss the back of your neck,

twirling an escaped strand of hair,
a dangling participle,
around my finger.

You are lost to me in daylight,
separate, unlike the night,
where you surrender

your darkness, calling
out the memory
of someone else's name.

Orchard Beach

Once, you say,
taking my arm, an apple orchard
blossomed here, replaced now
by imported sand and boardwalk.
Strolling into the quiet season
of autumn, we pause, leaning
against the rail, our thoughts
searching the hidden horizon.

Once, you point,
you hung out over there,
with the Italian kids, the Puerto Rican
kids beyond the bay, all of you sporting
the slicked back hair of insolent youth,
scouting territory and death with devilish dares,
life thrilling and loitering before you.
Now, today, half of you retired cops,
half of you in prison, equal halves of you dead.

Once, you reminisce,
you sold candy apples here,
this railing lacquered to a high varnish,
lustrous and gleaming, back then. Now,
painted over and over, layer over layer
of dull brown paint comes off
in large cracked chips, leaving
deep pockets where wood grain
still glows, like long ago.

Once, I tell you,
I was shaken by the crack,
of your exposed rage, layered
deeply, now, under old wounds.
I tasted the tart, bitterness of yesterday
on your lips, like a candy apple
covered with a fiery hard red coating,
disguising the sweetness inside.

Once again,
you guide my arm, the staccato beat
of our steps accompanied by a soprano
seagull's solo. I can already hear
you pacing, searching in the middle
of darkness for tomorrow's dream,
until frustrated you return to sleep,
my hand finding yours for the journey.

Unnecessary Junk

My brain bolted out of the bank today,
infuriated after I stuffed her into my purse.
She deserved punishment,
embarrassing me by pulling

the check, I had sworn to the teller
was deposited last week, right out
of my satchel. She began leaving
without notice, at the most inconvenient

moments, the day I decided to move,
and threatened to disappear forever
if I lost my glasses one more time.
Just yesterday, she snuck down the street,

climbed up the wooden post to the mailbox,
and grabbed four days of crunched, cramped mail.
Evading my grasp, she bounced
down the street to the pay phone,

canceling my electricity, phone, newspapers,
and garbage collection, knowing I'd forgotten.
Sulking at the bottom of my purse, beneath
my wallet, cosmetic bag, ungraded papers,

vitamins, and a torn-in-half self-help book
I'd piled upon her to really keep her down,
she busted loose. Stopped by security
as a suspicious blob, she returned arrogantly,

yet somewhat apologetic, knowing I couldn't
live without her. As I made her promise never
to leave me again, she laughed, haughty
and hearty as ever, and started to clean house.

She deleted all past guilts, rejections, fears
and loneliness, leaving only enough room
for the present moment, until, exhausted,
she wept, having finally destroyed

all the unnecessary junk I'd forced
her to carry around for far too many years.

Fantasy Fest (The Morning After)
by
Mary Alice Herbert

Mary-Alice Herbert

Mary-Alice Herbert is a late-blooming poet, playwright, and publisher who has been living and working on Sugarloaf Key, near Key West for seven years. Her poetry publications include *Barefoot Journal*, *Solares Hill*, *Key West Celebrate*, *Spectrum* (The Literary Magazine of the Florida Keys Community College), and *Rattle*. "Grandpap", a three-act play, was read at the Waterfront Playhouse, Key West.

Fantasy Fest (The Morning After)*

Fantasy Fest, Key West
is all about the breast.
It's celebration time for
bosoms, hooters, tits and toots.
I've been coming out in stages
year by year, casting off
a few more inhibitions
and a few more clothes.
But until just yesterday, my breasts
were too uptight to play.

A pirate for a partner, I
dress up as a wench,
in chemise, chemisette
petticoats, beribboned
bodice, a garland
of gentle pansies in my hair.
I suck in and hold 'em high,
I heave and mold, I lace
and lace again, until
my boundless beauties rise,
barely tipped in lace!

I don a mask.
We hit the streets,
"Oh, Momma!"
(we've hardly left the parking lot)
"Oh, let me take your picture!"
On Duval Street
A little boy no more than thirty winks
"I like your shirt!"

Another about twice his age
gapes goggle-eyed
"Oh, fuck, they're real!"
Women tell me I look cute.
They call me "Honey"
More times in an hour
than I've heard in all my life.
"Oh, my God!" "Sweet Jesus!"
I move some men to prayer.

Later at The Rooftop
the waiter croons,
"You look mah-ve-lous!"
An angel in a merry-widow
(white satin beaded bustier)
beats his wings and sighs.
A chocolate beauty
in pink satin tap pants
(his puppies nestle in a pink brassiere)
sings out
"You go, girl. Work it! Work it!"

Below me, down on Front Street
after sunset fades
the parade begins
and, Honey, this girl is hot.
She spills over the balustrade,
waves and works it
earns her beads.
How sweet those shining jewels!
They rise high, they arch
and they come flying home
to rest upon these breasts.

* Fantasy Fest is Key West's annual Mardi Gras & Halloween Party

Galway Bay & other poems
By Daniel Spinella

Daniel Spinella

Daniel Spinella was born in New York at Coney Island Hospital... in the shadow of the Cyclone. He has studied poetry with Paul Hoover, Galway Kinnell, and Molly Peacock, and visual arts—and Neil Young—are also lasting influences. He is still a sometime photographer (or sometimes a still photographer).

His poems and reviews have appeared in a number of small press magazines. He has also been featured on Dial-a-Poem Chicago on three occasions. His chapbook of poetry, *Looking for Signs of Life in the Universe*, was published before Tomlin. He is currently working on a chapbook of poems on Buffalo Bill and the Wild West Show.

Edison's First Film

Bill sits stiff legged on horseback, sunlight
around the old man and camera flare,
stained duster dirty boots
at the head of a parade,
not fluid as the Plains, dark eyes
under a large brim starless
cloud above a lake,

thin wind across Nebraska
catching steers with winter
in their throats. He chokes
on arena dust, whirled and
galloped cowgirls, Cossacks,
cavalry, vaqueros, caracoling
ground for the created Cody.

A one camera setup hinged
on a tripod, flat light ghosts
the motion, its operator
chews Redman, cranks steady.

Galway Bay

Missing Persons

In Dublin I search for missing persons.
I count the shadows on O'Connell Bridge,
pose queries to the Gardia
at the General Post Office,
gossip in pubs on Grafton Street.
From a long way off I hear

the sound of an old man coughing,
a Maxwell House coffee tin
by his bed, his wife
resting quietly in the next room,
surrounded by images of
St. Anthony and the Infant
under glass. I press my face

against a window.
Brown box elevated trains
roar by. "You can see
those trains?" my grandmother asks.
"You must have good eyes." I can see
anything that will take me away.

I take a train to Dublin
to Galway City. And when I get there
I look out on the bay to see
Agnes Mulaney boarding
a ship to the new world,
for a life as cheerless
as the North Atlantic.

Lengthening Shadow

The mute swans of Galway City rest
in mud flats, sleeping near the earth.
A red trawler ties up at Irish Shell.
"Here's one for your camera...
a lovely cloud pink
as a salmon." The old fellow
pulls on his cigarette.
His spaniels roust terns.
Stone erupts like language from the earth,
good for building houses, sheltering animals,
capturing pools of water. As I walk, the air
feels coarse and damp.
Brown seaweed fans out along
the beach like lung tissue.
Over the ocean the lengthening shadow
of a squall is as blue as breath.

A Note from Emma Hutchinson to Col. Cody Concerning the 1,000-Mile Cowboy Race

June 1893

Dear Col. Cody,

I understand now. My luck against
Buffalo Bill's 1,000 groundsmen. This fortnight
I leave for fair Chadron. My only feed

simple fare. A little milk each day
to toughen the simplest miles. My ponies,
the finest Sioux racers, bred like blood-thirsty
death. *Race Outlaw* the horse to win,
Crow Endurance, Mankiller.

I am counting on seeing you
in 20 days, Col. Cody, in pearl-handled Chicago.
A new Colt's, gold inlaid, $1,000, and a fine cowboy

saddle waiting, not for riding in town
but for the open range.

Yours,
Emma Hutchinson

MIDNIGHT MIND NUMBER TWO

THREE
POEMS
BY
JEFF VANDE ZANDE

Jeff Vande Zande

Jeff Vande Zande lives with his wife and son in Lower Michigan where he teaches English at Delta College. His poetry and short stories have appeared in over thirty small press magazines and journals, including *College English*, *Passages North*, *Green Hills Literary Lantern*, *The MacGuffin*, and *Fugue*. Two of his poems were nominated for the 1999 Pushcart Prize. In June of 2001, March Street Press released his chapbook of poems entitled *Transient*. In addition he is the poetry editor of *The Driftwood Review*.

Sundown

As though marking time,
fly rods swing
above the gray-haired men.
Their eyes adjust slowly
to the fading light.

Late season nymphs emerge,
mayflies drying into first flight.
Having clung to the stony river bottom,
the insects linger above the water,
mourning a mother
that now would drown them.

Standing against the strong current,
the men pause
to watch fingerling trout,
small rainbows breaking the surface,
foolish with hunger and life.

When bats skip low
across the river, the men recall
wristing roofing shingles
in a vacant lot. "It's really not
that dark," one says.
A mayfly's tiny legs
tangle briefly in his eyelashes.

Back at the tents, neither talks
of sleep. One follows a flashlight,
searches for kindling.
The other, finding a match,
scrapes a flame out of stone.

In the Basement

He feels his way
through the dark halls, hands slipping
along the walls and down

the banister. In the aquarium,
the fish feel the rhythm of his feet
and pop hungry kisses at the surface.

Down the second flight of stairs
he waits for the sulfur to chill him
like a ghost, but it's never there.

He remembers his father, his race home
every Friday night to remind himself
why he worked outdoors all week,

awake and asleep in the cold woods.
How could his mother have known what he'd do
the weekend she took the boys to Duluth.

Sometimes, twisting light
into the single bulb overhead,
he'll see the body again in the corner

until his eyes adjust and he steps up
onto the treadmill. Marching
against the constant belt,

he usually forgives his father, the exercise
giving him time to think, like a long night
alone in acres of cruised timber.

MIDNIGHT MIND NUMBER TWO

He stares at himself in the ground floor window,
already buried, jogging nowhere in soil,
small roots splintered through his skull.

Some mornings the image is clear,
and the faint luminescence flickers
until he feels ready to stop running.

Upstairs, though, the joists and walls
pulse with his family's waking,
and his children soon find him risen,

in the kitchen, his face a sweating stone,
his resolved lips sipping coffee
at first light.

We Watched, We Waited

Our father had to retire early,
and, spending that first summer at camp,
we looked for green frogs around the bayou.
Once, we found a carp swaying in the reeds,
drifted up from the bottom
of the black drop-off, water
we always dared each other to swim in.

When we told my father, he stopped coughing
and grabbed a dusty net off the wall,
said the dead body was perfect bait
for his old crayfish trap, a trick
we watched him row out into the lake.
No life jacket, he stood in the boat,
lowered the chicken wire box by rope
into the thick, shadowy water.

The other end was knotted
through an old milk jug's handle,
a marker for the morning, anchored
against an evening of whitecaps.
We watched him jump off the bow
into the shallows and drag
the boat half way up the shore by himself.

He told us we'd sleep on the beach
that night, around a campfire he'd build.
In the last gray of dusk,
he handed out a beer to each of us,
and then he talked
about the next morning's haul, our catch
of freshwater "lobster", dropped
into boiling water – tails and claws
reddened, cracked, and dipped in butter.

MIDNIGHT MIND NUMBER TWO

For hours we forgot the clockwork
cadence of the waves. We
listened to our father's laugh wild like the flames,
our backs turned to the blackness.
After the logs burned down to embers,
my father stood, waved off the flashlight,
and walked down the shoreline.
We watched the darkness shroud his silhouette,
leaving only the cherry of his cigarette
dancing against the rhythm of the breakers.

THE GUIDE TO SAFE CAMPING

Camping Tip #3

GOOD *vs.* BAD

ENGLISH MUFFINS *vs.* BREAD

When packing food into your backpack, bread has a tendency to get smashed down into something that would better be used to play catch. English muffins, however, stay shapely and give a domesticated feel to your camping trip.

WATER FILTER *vs.* BACTERIA INFECTION

Two stories: The first is you shelling out $49.99 for the latest, greatest water filter at REI. Sounds bad? Second story. You hooked up to an I.V. after four straight days of staring at the three square feet in front of your toilet. $50 never seemed like such a good investment.

WHISKEY *vs.* BEER

Whiskey is light with the weight but heavy on the effectiveness. Beer? Too heavy for a backpack and you piss most of it away anyway.

CLEAN SOCKS *vs.* NO SOCKS

$A \times 2 \times 2 = B$

A = the # of socks you think you need.
B = the # of socks you actually need.

PAPERBACK *vs.* HARDCOVER

Although you might be generally fascinated with that wall of hardcover books at your apartment, leave them there when camping. Paperbacks are lighter and cost less to replace if your book becomes toilet paper or kindling. Besides, your hardcover copy of *Fletch Lives* could be lost to a heavy rain or river crossing and then what would you do?

AND ONE INTERVIEW...

FRESHWATER FISH

brook trout

rock bass

bluegill sunfish

yellow perch

muskellunge

walleyed pike

catfish

largemouth bass

Behind the Mind of
Chris Dombrowski
Interviewed by Julie Dunn, freelance journalist for *The New York Times*.

March 18th, 2001

Chris Dombrowski is a poet living in Missoula, Montana. He graduated from Hope College with a degree in English and his teaching certificate in secondary education. In May, he will receive his M.F.A. in creative writing with a focus on poetry from the University of Montana. His work has been published in the *Crab Creek Review*, a literary magazine out of Seattle, the *Talking River Review* of Lewiston, Idaho, and *Midnight Mind Number One*. His poem "Answer to My Mother" was a winner in the Atlantic Monthly Student Writer Competition. Below are excerpts from our phone interview, me in my East Village apartment, picturing him in the Missoula winter, with a smile on his face.

You can read Dombrowski's poetry in *Midnight Mind Number One*.

Q. What is your favorite piece?
A. My favorite poem is always my next poem. I love the work, the discovery, and it seems that whatever I wrote today seems old two weeks from now.

Q. Are you more inspired when you are out and about in the world, or do you have to be focusing specifically on writing?
A. I'm more inspired when I sit down to write. Rodin said something like: "I have no time for inspiration," by which he meant, I think, that if you sit around waiting for inspiration, you'll do a lot of not working. He also believed that the best art comes out of objectivity and that inspiration doesn't always breed this objectivity. That said, I get a lot of ideas from walking around, being in the world. I believe in the importance of individual experience, so I try to strike a balance between being a bookhead and being in the world. In the end, though, nothing happens if you don't sit down and do it.

Q. WHEN DID YOU WRITE YOUR FIRST POEM?
A. I wrote these two songs when I was 5 or 6. One is about these older boys at the bus stop, sitting around without coats on. It's winter, it's freezing, I'm looking at them wondering why they don't put scarves on. The other is about the half-moon, a very melancholy, typically romantic vision. Maybe that contrast is the root of my writing.

Q. WHO DO YOU ENJOY READING?
A. I read everything. I try to read voraciously, that's my motto. I read things I don't expect to like. There are a few poets I read over and over again, who constantly amaze me, or upset me. Jim Harrison is one of them. He considers his poetry his life work, considers the novels just tacked on. That's saying lot. He's so inventive with his poetry. His influences include Whitman, Lorca, Neruda, Rimbaud. They're noticeable, but not overbearing in his work.

Q. WHO DO YOU CONSIDER INFLUENTIAL?
A. In some ways, everything I read is somewhat influential, but I love old Haiku, and the T'ang Dynasty poets. I love Wordsworth, Rimbaud. Larry Levis is a contemporary poet who I admire. But I learn, and am influenced, by everything I read, and by my teachers and peers.

Q. AS AN ACTIVE OUTDOORSMAN, ARE YOU MORE INFLUENCED BY MALE AUTHORS WITH SIMILAR INTERESTS?
A. It does sound like I'm mentioning only male authors, doesn't it? Wallace Stevens said, "Worst of all things is not to live in a physical world." I like poets who inhabit the physical world–whatever exactly that means–Elizabeth Bishop, Sharon Olds, Gallway Kinnell–there is a book I

read recently by a Swedish born poet, Malena Morling, that is a fantastic example of living in a physical world. But to answer your question, I think good art is pretty androgynous.

Q. DO YOU EVER WRITE IN A FEMALE VOICE? DO YOU THINK THAT MALE WRITERS CAN ACCURATELY SEE LIFE FROM A WOMAN'S POINT OF VIEW?
A. That's a great question. I try it every now and then. Stevens' "Sunday Morning" is certainly a great example of doing this successfully. There are millions of other examples too. Right now I'm looking at a photo of my grandmother, it's above my desk. I have this poem that I've written that comes out of her head, but even then it's not writing in her voice, it's covering up my own. I've set a few poems in feminine voices, but I think you're just masking your own voice, which in the end can be pretty cool.

Q. DO YOU THINK THE CURRENT MINDSET OF NOT TEACHING ERNEST HEMINGWAY PASSES OVER GREAT LITERATURE JUST TO BE POLITICALLY CORRECT?
A. I think Hemingway is a great writer. Say what you want about his politics. If you read his sentences, they aren't sexist, they're good. And sure, he may have been, along with some of his characters, an asshole, but I think you can learn as much about humanity from an asshole or a sexist as you can from any upstanding citizen.

Q. IF YOU HAD TO PUBLISH A BOOK TOMORROW, WHAT WOULD YOU TITLE IT?
A. The other day I told my friend I might call my manuscript of poems, *In the Valley of Rough Gods*. He said that

was pretty lame, that I could do better. We were fishing, though, and I was watching the herons. I have a list of about 50 bad titles. Is it better to have no title or a shitty title? A lot of people ask, What is the value of getting an MFA? Why don't you just go out into the world and write? Because the world doesn't want you to write–the world wants you to work, run a business, take kids to basketball practice. Grad school gives you two or three years to get your momentum going. It gives you time to get some of the bad work out of your system, the 50 bad titles.

Q. How many poems have you written about fish?
A. So few, but I'm proud of the ones that I've written. I've written three poems about fishing. I really made an effort to not do that, because I felt that I was pushing myself into a corner. I do write a lot about rivers. It's funny. I gave a reading the other night and the person was going to introduce me as "the fishing poet" and I said, "that's bullshit, I never write about fish." But people who know me....

MIDNIGHT MIND NUMBER TWO

Submission Policy

The Midnight Mind journals are published in March and September of each year. To submit for work review, send it to the following to the address:

White Fish Press
Midnight Mind journal
PO Box 1131
New York, NY
10003

Please check the web site for upcoming projects.

To submit via email attach a word document and email to info@MidnightMind with the subject "Midnight Mind Journal Submission"

Please be sure that all submissions include your full mailing address and email address. All entries must be typed, double-spaced, and in a common font. Comic Sans is not a common font.

Send us letters & we will like you.

You can email letters to us at info@WhiteFishPress.com or send letters to us at the same address as above.

Some general rules:
1. If you are refering to someone we do not know, please try to send a picture.
2. If you are refering to someone we do know, speak kindly, unless, of course, we do not like them either.
3. If you are writing to tell us about how you recently purchased an old Jeep CJ-7, talk long, and in detail, as we are already interested.

EDITOR'S NOTE - ON CAMPING AND BOOKS...

I must admit, first, that these are two of my favorite things along with fishing, cars, and islands. I have been camping for as long as I can remember. First, out in our backyard and woods in Portage, Michigan and in northern Michigan. Then, I continued in places like Key West, upstate New York, Nantucket, and the shore of the Atlantic. And all these places retain their charm in my memory.

When I was ten or eleven, I started out with Boy Scout Troop 243, where my brother had blazed the way enough for me to already have friends in Scouts, and it seems that this was my camping peak. Over the third five-year period of my life, I camped all across the United States and did all sorts of camping.

Out on the road with the Scouts, I fell in love with camping for the first time. It was also where I fell "in love" for the first time. I met her at a KOA somewhere outside of Denver. The campground had a water slide and go-carts. I talked to her after we raced each other in the go-carts. She was 15 (maybe) and I told her lies about how I played football. She was beautiful and I could not shake the visions of her and I alone in a tent (which, of course, never happened). The lies worked, though, and we hung out all night and listened to *Stairway to Heaven* until a neighboring camper yelled for us to go to sleep. In the months after, we wrote each other until my lies of being a football player were exposed through a cousin she had who lived in a town to the south of us. It was the first time I learned the world was smaller than you think.

I can remember a specific KOA alongside of the highway out in what must have been Kansas. We could hear the roar of the diesel trucks motoring through the night while we tried to sleep in our two-person tents. Across from this site was an old museum dealing with the history of oilrigs and oil drilling. A mid-fifties pick-up truck that had been rigged for driving pipe into the ground sat rusting out in the front lawn of the museum, the weeds grown wild around its flat, worthless tires.

No one else except Paul (my tent-mate) and I took an interest in the old beat-up truck rusting there. Paul and I walked over to look at it. The door was unlocked and we got inside and sat. The museum seemed closed, possibly it had not been open in a long time. But we sat there and acted as if we were oil riggers, Paul

DIATELY A THOUSAND MILES FROM MYSELF. THERE HAVE BEEN A FEW MOMENTS IN MY LIFE THAT I WILL ALWAYS REMEMBER AND THAT IS ONE OF THEM. I AM NOT SURE I CAN ACHIEVE THAT FEELING OF RELAXATION AGAIN, OF ONENESS WITH MYSELF. IT WAS THE COMING TOGETHER OF TWO NEW IDEAS (READING AND CAMPING) THAT I WOULD CONTINUE TO DO AS LONG AS I COULD.

THE SAD THING IS THAT THE BOOK DID NOT LAST LONG. I LOST IT TOWARD THE END OF THE TRIP BUT NOT BEFORE I WAS ABLE TO SPEND TIME READING IT WHILE CAMPING.

CAMPING OVER THE YEARS, FOR ME, HAS COME IN TWO FORMS:

1. ACTUAL CAMPING
2. CAMPING VIA THE ARMCHAIR

"CAMPING VIA THE ARMCHAIR" WAS INTRODUCED TO ME FIRST BY *The Boy Scout Handbook* AND TO THIS DAY COMES IN FORMS OF KNOT-TYING BOOKS THAT I BUY DUE TO MY INABILITY TO MEMORIZE PROPER FISHING KNOTS. I AM ALSO PARTIAL TO THE MODERN BOOKS OF JON KRAKAUER (*Into Thin Air*, *Into the Wild*), AND THE CLASSICS OF LOUIS L'AMOUR AND GUESS WHO, ZANE GREY. APPLES DON'T FALL FAR FROM THE TREE AS MY GRANDFATHER READ LOUIS L'AMOUR AS IF IT WERE THE OLD

DRIVING AND MYSELF LEANING BACK RELAXING IN THE PASSENGER SEAT AFTER A HARD DAY'S DRILLING. AT SOME POINT I OPENED THE GLOVE COMPARTMENT AND PULLED OUT AN OLD HARDCOVER COPY OF A ZANE GREY BOOK. THE BOOK WAS AN OLD HARDCOVER, DUSTY AND BRITTLE, BUT IN MY EYES, BEAUTIFUL. I WAS ABSOLUTELY AMAZED AND HAD VISIONS THAT THE BOOK BELONGED TO SOMEONE ON THE PRAIRIE — THAT I HELD IN MY HANDS THE BOOK THAT SOMEONE ELSE WHO HAD REALLY CAMPED (BEFORE THE DIESEL TRUCKS AND WATERSLIDES) HAD HELD IN THEIR HANDS. THERE WAS NOTHING I COULD DO BUT TAKE IT.

THIS MIGHT BE THE FIRST TIME THE WORLD OF BOOKS, AND THEREFORE READING, MIXED WITH A TENT, THE SMELL OF FEET, AND AN UNROLLED SLEEPING BAG.

I REMEMBER A FEELING I HAD. THIS WAS WHILE WE WERE ACTUALLY HIKING AND CAMPING OUT AT THE PHILMONT RANCH IN NEW MEXICO LATER THAT SAME TRIP. WE HAD BEEN A FEW DAYS OUT AND WE WERE TIRED. WE GOT INTO CAMP EARLY AND SET UP OUR TENTS. THE AFTERNOON WAS STILL STRONG WITH LIGHT BUT THE HEAT WAS COMFORTABLE. I GOT INTO THE TENT AND THE LIGHT COMING THROUGH THE TAN TENT SIDE CAST A RELAXING LIGHT. I LAID DOWN ON MY SLEEPING BAG AND FELT THE FEW DAYS OF HIKING DRAIN FROM MY LEGS. I STARTED TO READ THE ZANE GREY BOOK AND WAS IMME-

"ACTUAL CAMPING." CAMPING IS GETTING OUTDOORS, ENJOYING THE WEATHER (BAD OR GOOD), HIKING, SWIMMING AND MAKING FOOD (SOMETIMES A HUGE PROCESS IN ITS OWN RIGHT, SEE GLOSSARY OF TERMS "RAMEN NOODLES").

ON A RECENT CAMPING TRIP, MY GIRLFRIEND, A BUNCH OF MY BEST FRIENDS, AND MYSELF SET OUT INTO THE LOW MOUNTAINS NORTHEAST OF SEATTLE (NEAR SKYKOMISH) TO TRY TO HIKE WHAT LOOKED LIKE A RELATIVELY EASY TRAIL. I SAY "RELATIVELY" BECAUSE WHAT WAS AN EASY HIKE TURNED INTO A MOSQUITO-FILLED HIKE FROM HELL.

SOMEONE GOT THE IDEA TO BRING THE FISHING POLES WHICH, AFTER THE LONG (WAY TOO LONG) HIKE UP THE MOUNTAIN (AND IT DID TURN OUT TO BE A MOUNTAIN), ENDED UP BEING LEFT BEHIND AT ONE OF OUR BREAK POINTS. WE HAD TWO DOGS WITH US AND BOTH WERE COMIC RELIEF FOR THE TRIP, BUT ON THE HIKE IT BECAME A SPECTACLE. ONE DOG, JACK, WOULD RACE AHEAD OF EVERYONE THEN RUN BACK TO SEE HIS THAT HIS OWNER, JAMIE WALTER, WAS OKAY AND THEN RACE AHEAD AGAIN. THE OTHER DOG, HOWEVER, A YELLOW LAB, LET'S JUST CALL HIM "BIG GUY",

THIS IS NOT "BIG GUY"

TESTAMENT.

SOME OF THE BEST ARMCHAIR CAMPING COMES IN THE FORM OF A TALL GLASS OF WATER, A COMFORTABLE CHAIR AND THE SLEEK PAGES OF THE LATEST PATAGONIA CATALOG. THIS CATALOG, WHILE ADVERTISING FOR THE PATAGONIA CLOTHING COMPANY, CAN SOMETIMES BE A CAMPING VACATION JUST READING IT. THE PHOTOGRAPHY IS UP THERE WITH ANY COFFEE TABLE BOOK, AND THE PHOTOS TAKE YOU TO PLACES THAT CAMPERS DREAM OF (HANGING OFF THE SIDE OF A CLIFF WHILE MAKING COFFEE IN YOUR TENT, A GREAT SHOT OF A TENT SET ON ROCKS OVERLOOKING THE EXPANSE OF WATERFALLS OF SOME DISTANT LAND). THE GEAR IN THESE CATALOGS (AS WELL AS THE MORE GEAR-ORIENTED LL BEAN, CAMPMOR, AND CABELA'S) MAKE THE ARMCHAIR SEEM SUDDENLY UNCOMFORTABLE. THAT PERHAPS YOUR HEART RATE SHOULD BE UP AND YOUR CONCERN SHOULD BE FIGURING OUT A CONVENIENT PLACE TO KEEP YOUR WATER BOTTLE IN YOUR BACKPACK SO THAT YOU CAN GRAB IT ON THE HIKE W/O SLOWING DOWN.

BUT LET'S GET DOWN TO THE BRASS TACKS HERE.

ALARM CLOCK IS ABSENT, DIDN'T STIR AS I GOT OUT OF THE TENT. THE MORNING WAS COLD AND THE SKY WAS JUST BEGINNING TO GET LIGHT, ALTHOUGH THE SUN WAS A FEW HOURS AWAY FROM RISING OVER THE PEAKS.

I FOUND A BUSH AND RELIEVED MYSELF, MY BREATH STEAMING IN THE COLD. I THOUGHT THEN HOW TRULY DIFFERENT CAMPING CAN MAKE YOUR LIFE SEEM. I WORK IN NEW YORK CITY WHERE I WAKE UP EVERY MORNING TO STREET NOISE, GARBAGE TRUCKS, HORNS, YELLING, AND/OR CONSTRUCTION. I GET ON THE 4 TRAIN OR THE A,C, OR E AND TAKE IT UP TO "MIDTOWN" TO THE OFFICE. THEN I SIT IN A CUBE MADE FROM WHAT APPEARS TO BE CORK BOARD WITH LITTLE SPIRALS ON IT. THERE IS NOT A WINDOW IN SIGHT OF MY CUBE. I HAVE TO WALK INTO SOMEONE ELSE'S OFFICE JUST TO SEE WHAT THE WEATHER IS DOING. ARE WE REALLY MEANT TO LIVE THIS WAY? WHAT ABOUT UNZIPPING YOUR TENT, GRABBING A BOOK FROM YOUR BACKPACK (WHERE ALL YOUR POSSESSIONS ARE EXCEPT THOSE IN THE BEAR BAG), AND TAKING A PISS IN THE BUSHES? WHAT ABOUT THE AIR? SHOULDN'T WE ALL BE ABLE TO BREATHE IN THIS FRESH AIR EVERYDAY?

SO THAT WAS MY MINDSET AS I SAT DOWN BY THE RIVER AND READ. I WAS READING *Rivethead: Tales from the Assembly Line* BY BEN HAMPER, ABOUT THE DEMISE OF FLINT, MICHIGAN AFTER GENERAL MOTORS PULLED OUT. THE TOWN WAS/IS IN

FOUGHT FOR EVERY INCH OF GROUND HE CLIMBED AND SEEMED TO MISS THE RELAXING SOLITUDE OF HIS CORNER OF THE COUCH. HE LAGGED BEHIND. HE WAS AFRAID TO CROSS THE WATER. WHEN ALL FINALLY ARRIVED AT THE BEAUTIFUL "ALPINE LAKE" ATOP THE CLIMB, WE WERE SWARMED BY MOSQUITOES SO BIG AND HUNGRY THAT EVEN "BIG GUY" WAS ABLE TO GET DOWN THE MOUNTAIN AT A QUICK PACE.

ONCE BACK DOWN WE RELAXED, COOKED OUR RAMEN NOODLES, PUMPED CLEAN WATER, WASHED PLATES IN THE FREEZING COLD WATER, AND SAT AROUND THE FIRE. IN OTHERS WORDS - CAMPED. REAL CAMPING. NOT SLEEPING IN THE BACK OF A VAN OR SLEEPING NEXT TO YOUR CAR OR JUST DOWN FROM THE PEOPLE WHO BROUGHT THE HAMMOCK, THE AMERICAN FLAG, A 12-PACK OF MOUNTAIN DEW, TRICYCLES FOR THE KIDS, ETC, ETC, ETC. WE WERE FIVE MILES FROM OUR CAR, WHERE CELL PHONES GET NO SIGNAL, WHERE YOU PUT BEAR BAGS UP IN THE TREES BEFORE YOU GO TO SLEEP. AND YOU SLEEP SOUNDLY: THE SLEEP OF A MAN WHO HAD TO WORK FOR THIS SOFT PATCH OF GROUND WITHIN EARSHOT OF A RUNNING RIVER.

WE SLEPT SOUNDLY THAT NIGHT. THE ONLY ODD NOISE I HEARD WAS "BIG GUY" GETTING UP TO PEE IN THE WOODS, HIS DOG CHAIN TINKLING AS HE PASSED OUR TENTS.

IN THE MORNING I WOKE EARLIER THAN EVERYONE ELSE. MY GIRLFRIEND, WHO SLEEPS UNTIL NOON WHEN AN

shambles and acres of land lay covered with boarded up factories, homes, stores. "Buick City", which was once the pride of General Motors and Flint and Michigan is now a cinder block museum of bad corporate planning, decisions, ideas. The result of answering to stockholders and not a community or even a country. And it struck me as odd that I was reading about this place in a completely different world. A place of beauty untouched by corporations or factories or stockholders. And again it became one of those moments in my life that became clear. One of those moments I will remember forever. What blended this time? Reading, camping and a personal philosophy?

Eventually everyone else began to wake up. The dogs began running around like wild animals, leaving broken tree branches in their wake, piss marks, and shrubbery dragging from their tails. I wandered back into the campsite for breakfast. We were leaving that morning and wanted to get a good start so we didn't waste the afternoon in the truck. All of us sat around the camp stove and cooked our remaining food. One friend excused himself to go to the bathroom in the woods.

We took down our tent and the friend who went out to the bathroom returned, mumbled, asked for the shovel, and went back out. Ah, the joys of camping. I tucked the book back into my backpack. Everyone was ready to leave so we started hiking, the dogs, fresh with energy, leading the way.

A little way down the trail, the friend who had gone the bathroom in the woods dropped back to talk to me. "Something strange happened back there in the woods."

"What?"

"I went back to cover my crap and it was gone."

"Gone?"

"Yeah."

Then we were both quiet.

"The dogs you think?"

He sighed. "Big Guy" was his dog.

"Which one?" I asked.

"I don't know. But one of them for sure."

We were each trying to talk over the sound of our backpacks. The trees were just starting to let the direct sunlight through.

"Can't wait to get back to the real world, you know?" He said.

"Yeah. I know."

Enjoy the book.

-Brett van Emst
Editor

Glossary of Terms

Boy Scout Water *or Gasoline* / boi skaut woter / n, [MF, prob. ger. ONF or OProv, fr.] (1865) 1. A: a volatile, flammable liquid hydrocarbon mixture used as a fuel to start camp fires. usu. used with large pile of small sticks, fallen trees limbs, or store bought split hardwood. B: liquid used to start camp fires i.e. "bring that can of - over here and get this fire going".

Bud Light / bood-e-lee-tay *or* bud lit / n, attrib [MF, prob. amer. anheuser busch, amer. L. *buddis litis* beer, life] (1828) 1. A: an alcoholic beverage usu. made from malted cereal (usually barley, in this case something less) and lots of water. B: most often used as a muscle relaxer during camping or in the car on the way to camp, i.e. "now that we are driving, pass me a cold can of - to begin the relaxing weekend".

Camp / kamp / n, [MF, prob. fr. ONF or OProv, fr. L. *campus* plain, field] (1892) 1 A: a place usu. away from urban areas where tents or simple buildings (as cabins) are erected for shelter or temporary residence (as for laborers, prisoners or vacationers) B: a group of tents, cabins, or huts i.e. "fishing -s along the river".

Camper / kamper / n, [MF, prob. fr. ONF or OProv, fr. L. *campimus*] (1528) 1. A: a person usu. away from urban areas in the act of setting up or enjoying camp. (usu. for laborers, prisoners or vacationers. spring breakers) B: a shoe C: "damn -s dump their trash in the roads".

Camp Fire / kamp-fir / n, (1675) 1. A: a fire built outdoors.

Car Camping / kaar kampin / v, [amer. L. *coach campus* auto, coach, fold down trunk] (1955) 1. A: the act of camping usu. in areas (as state parks, mountains regions) where an automobile (car, truck, hippy van) is used for shelter (as for road-weary travelers, poor travelers or MFA students) B: used often in case of bad weather and destruction of tent, cabin, or structured shelter, i.e. "the tent is leaking, on the count of three, run for the car, tonight we are -".

Grasser / gras-uhr / n, [amer. L. *grassus partus*] (1950). often attrib to the older generation [MF, prob. fr. OGF or OProv, back forty. L. *Grassus* field] (1964) 1. A: a place of camping in old fields or back lawns of party hosts. Outdated term. B: "my dad used to get bands from chicago to come out and play his -s".

KEGGER / KEGG-UHR / N, OFTEN ATTRIB TO COLLEGE STUDENTS [MF, PROB. FR. OAF OR OPROV, FR. L. *Keggus*. BEER, TAP, FOAM] (1528) 1. A: SIMILAR TO GRASSER WITH THE DIFFERENCE BEING KEGGERS TAKE PLACE ANYWHERE AND ONLY SOMETIMES INVOLVE CAMPING. B: "BETTER GET YOUR DRINKING SHOES ON, OVER ON ALBERT STREET, THEY ARE HAVING A -".

LED ZEPPLIN 4 / LED ZEEP-LYN / N, OFTEN ATTRIB [MF, PROB. FR. ONF OR OPROV, FR. L. *God guitairus*.] (1977) 1. A: WHEN CAMPING IN CAMPSITES, LED ZEPPLIN, MOST OFTEN LED ZEPPLIN 4, IS USED TO ATTRACT HUMAN COMPANIONSHIP. IF IN DANGER OF SPENDING THE NIGHT ALONE, RESORT TO *Stairway to Heaven*. B: "WANT TO COME OVER AND LISTEN TO -?".

MASS CAMPING / MASS KAMP-IN / N, OFTEN ATTRIB TO NEW JERSEY YOUTH [MF, PROB. FR. ONF OR OPROV, FR. L. *massus campus*, HOUSE, YARD, WOOD] (1982) A. CAMPING WITH MANY PEOPLE THAT YOU DO NOT DIRECTLY KNOW. B: MOST OFTEN WITNESSED AT HIGH SCHOOL "SENIOR PARTIES" AND PHISH CONCERTS.

PABST BLUE RIBBON / PAPST BLU REIB-UN / N, OFTEN ATTRIB TO WISCONSIN AND/OR PACKERS FANS [MF, PROB. FR. ONF OR OPROV, FR. L. *beerus goodus*, WHEAT, WATER] (1938) 1. THE NUMBER ONE DRINK FOR CAR CAMPING OR MASS CAMPING OR BIKER BARS. A: HAS THE ABILITY TO RE-HYDRATE YOU WHILE STILL CAUSING INTOXICATION. B: NOTED BY THE WHIMSICAL AND FUN TO SAY, "PBR ME ASAP" AND NEAT OLD-TIME LABEL.

RAMEN NOODLES / ROM-IN NOO-DELS / N, OFTEN ATTRIB TO THE POOR OR LAZY [MF, PROB. FR. ONF OR OPROV, FR. L. *eatus slopdis*. FOOD, AMER. CUSINE] (1976) 1. A: NOODLES WITH 200% DAILY RECOMMENDED AMOUNT OF SODIUM. AVERAGE COST =.21 CENTS A PACK (1/2 MEAL PER PACK) A STAPLE OF THE CAMPING DIET (THIS INCLUDES ALL TYPES OF CAMPING). B: USED AS A CHECK BETWEEN CAMPERS AS TO THEIR CAMPING EXPERIENCE I.E. "EVER EATEN THE SHRIMP-FLAVORED -?".

PITCH-A-TENT PARTY / PITSCH A TINT PAR-TE / N, OFTEN ATTRIB TO IRISH CAMPERS [MF, PROB. FR. ONF OR OPROV, FR. L. *campus suburbis*, BACK YARD] (1998) 1. A: A PLACE USU. IN URBAN AREAS WHERE TENTS ARE SET AS TEMPORARY RESIDENCE FOR PARTYGOERS. B: A GROUP OF TENTS IN THE BACK YARD FOR USE ONCE THE PARTY ENDS (OR DURING) I.E. "GLAD WE DO NOT HAVE TO DRIVE HOME TONIGHT SINCE IT IS A -".

SHIT SANDWICHES / SHET SAND-WITCH-IS / N, [MF, PROB. FR. ONF OR OPROV, FR. L. *bowles movementus*, WASTE] (1997) 1. A: THE UNFORTUNATE OCCURRENCE OF DOGS EATING HUMAN FECES. THIS SHOULD NEVER BE INTENTIONAL BUT OFTEN HAPPENS BEFORE THE COVER OF HUMAN WASTE CAN BE COMPLETED. B: A STACK OF HUMAN EXCREMENT I.E. "YOUR DOG JUST ATE A –".

Featuring work by:

Audrianne Hill
Edward Serken
H.B. Schwass
Serena Cosmo
Jonathan Mayor
Tom Short
Shonda Buchanan
Deborah Schakel
Chris Dombrowski
Scott Boylston
Alison Hess

Photography by
Bryan David Griffith

Midnight Mind Number One
Goimg Home Again

Midnight Mind Number One

The first literary journal from the newly created MidnightMind / White Fish Press. The journal's theme of "Going Home Again" takes the reader deep into the heart of the writer.

ISBN 0-9667097-8-0
$7.00

white
fish
press

Midnight Mind
Number One

Going Home Again

I-94: A Collection of Southwest Michigan Writers

I-94
a collection of
southwest michigan writers

edited by
brett van emst

Featuring work by:

Audrianne Hill
Bonnie Flaig
Marsha Meyer
Barbara Spring
Marc Carls
Julie Stotz
Christine Phillips
Mary Louise Westbrook
Kerry L. Hansen
Joseph A. Fester
Bryan Vandermolen
Dave Wilson
Todd Koebke
Tara Barry
Randall P. Vande Water
Mary Blocksma
Jacqueline Carey
Tom Short
Kim Gehrke
Michael Martin
Anne Vandermolen
Ione Lake

I-94: A Collection of Southwest Michigan Writers

This collection brings together the writings of twenty-two authors from Southwest Michigan. Through poetry, fiction, and non-fiction, the authors express the deep literary heritage of Michigan literature that began with Ernest Hemingway and continues today.

ISBN 0-9667097-0-5
$12.00

white
fish
press

Available November 2001

white fish press

key west: a collection

writing about and inspired by the island of key west

edited by brett van emst

ISBN 0-9667097-4-8 $12.00

Featuring work by:

Fiction
Denise Lassetter
Thomas Bligh
Jane Eaton Hamilton
Dave Runyon
Edward Serken

Non-Fiction
Joy Castro
Donna Smith
Ann Boese
Lori De Milto

Poetry
Barbara Crooker
Justine Buisson
W. Dale Nelson
Catherine Daly
Stuart Dybek
Mary Kate Azcuy
Naomi Rachel

Sarah Brown Weitzman
Neil Carpathios
Bobbi Lurie
Elsa Colligan
Gianna Russo
Ken Anderson
Julie Kate Howard
Willa Schneberg
Rosanne G. Potter
Barbara Foster
Sally Naylor
Candace Black
June Nelson
James Doyle
Miles A. Coon
Davi Walders
E.W. Beals
Katharyn Howd Machan
Rochelle Lynn Holt
Biljana D. Obradovic
Olivia Diamond

Julia Older
Frederic Berthoff
Virginia Merritt
Katherine Murphy
Christine Swanberg
Joanne Seltzer
Joanne Whalen
Carole A Borges
Dorothy K. Fletcher
Robert Gregory
David Ray
Deborah Straw
Shelley Boyd Malone
Melissa Gurley Banck
Carol Barre
Nina Feirer
Francie Noyes
Sue Ament
Evelyn Livingston
Claire Keyes
Michael Cleary

featuring work by:

[an] Shapiro
[Ri]chard Foerster
[Jo]hn Grey
[Ka]ren Lindquist
[ ] Kates
[An]gela Mazaris
[Ro]bert Frazier
[St]anley H. Barkan
[Pa]mela A. Bakker
[De]borah DeNicola
[Ma]xine Susman
[G.] Tod Slone
[Bi]rgit Truex
[Ha]rold G. Harlow
[Je]nnifer Laura Johnson
[Ma]ry Kate Azcuy
[He]len Lawson
[Su]ellen Wedmore
[Ma]deleine Beckman
[Ly]n Lifshin
[M]argaret Rozga
[Dr.] Jose Gonzalez
[Ro]bin Magowan
[Al]ison Hess
[Sc]ott Boylston
[De]nnis Upper
[Bi]ll Brown
[B.]Z. Niditch
[D]orothy Duncan Burris
[Je]ffrey Johnson
[L.]A. St. Andrews
[Lo]uise I. Webster
[Do]nna Barrett
[Ma]rcia Lipson
[Na]ncy Kerrigan Jarasek
[Ne]il C. Fitzgerald
[Li]sa Colligan
[Li]savietta Ritchie
[M]ark Saba
[To]m Short
[Ke]vin King
[A.]M. Juster
[M]atthew Wolf
[S]usan Terris
[E]ric Levy

nantucket: a collection

writing about and inspired by the island of nantucket

Nantucket: A Collection is the latest in the "Locations" series that started in 1998 with *I-94: A Collection of Southwest Michigan Writers*. This new collection takes the reader into the hearts and minds of visitors and natives alike. Forty-five authors share their memories of Nantucket through poetry and fiction.

While there are many books dealing with Nantucket's rich history of whaling and sailing, this is the first to record the current state of this island in the Atlantic. *Nantucket: A Collection* fills that void with work by current writers from all over the United States as well as a few authors within biking distance of The Muse.

ISBN 0-9667097-9-9
$12.00

white
fish
press

Bryan David Griffith Fine Art Photography

Griffith's artwork was featured in
Midnight Mind Number One

See Griffith's artwork on the web at BDGProductions.com

FUTURE WHITE FISH PRESS BOOKS

THE OUTERBOROUGHS: COLLECTED CRIME FICTION FROM THE OUTSKIRTS OF NEW YORK CITY

APRIL 2002

NEW YORK CITY IS CLEANING UP. ON THE OUTSKIRTS, HOWEVER, THE OLD WAYS STILL RULE AND THE STREETS HAVE NEVER BEEN MORE ALIVE WITH STRANGE AND DANGEROUS CRIMINALS.

ISBN 0-9667097-1-3

MARTHA'S VINEYARD: A COLLECTION

JUNE 2002

THE FOURTH BOOK IN THE WHITE FISH PRESS "LOCATIONS" SERIES TAKES US TO THE ISLAND OF MARTHA'S VINEYARD. OVER TWENTY WRITERS SHARE THEIR EXPERIENCES AND CONNECTION TO THE ISLAND IN THIS GREAT COLLECTION.

ISBN 0-9667097-3-X

INDEPENDENT BOOKSTORES THAT CARRY WHITE FISH PRESS BOOKS...

NANTUCKET BOOKWORKS
NANTUCKET, MASSACHUSSETTS

CRANBERRY BOOK BARN
NORTH CARVER, MASSACHUSSETTS

THE BOOKMAN
GRAND HAVEN, MICHIGAN

JOHN ROLLINS BOOKSELLERS
KALAMAZOO, MICHIGAN
PORTAGE, MICHIGAN

BOOKSELLERS ON MAIN
HOLLAND, MICHIGAN

STUDENT BOOK STORE
EAST LANSING, MICHIGAN

THE SINGAPORE BOOKSHOP
SAUGATUCK, MICHIGAN

ATHENA BOOK SHOP
KALAMAZOO, MICHIGAN

GET REAL ART
NEW YORK CITY, NEW YORK

IF YOU CAN'T FIND WHAT YOU WANT AT THESE GREAT INDEPENDENT BOOKSELLERS, OUR BOOKS ARE ALSO AVAILABLE FOR ORDER AT ANY BARNES & NOBLE STORE, AS WELL AS AMAZON.COM AND BN.COM.

PLEASE FEEL FREE TO HARASS YOUR LOCAL BOOKSELLER INTO CARRYING OUR TITLES.

SUBSCRIPTIONS:

WE ARE HAPPY TO ANNOUNCE THAT WE WILL OFFER SUBSCRIPTIONS STARTING WITH MIDNGHT MIND MUMBER THREE. THE PRICES FOR SUBSCRIPTIONS ARE AS FOLLOWS:
1 YEAR [TWO ISSUES] - $10.00
2 YEARS [FOUR ISSUES] - $18.00

YOU MAY SUBSCRIBE BY SENDING A CHECK AND A NOTE STATING WHICH ISSUE TO START WITH: WHITE FISH PRESS, PO BOX 1131, NY. NY 10003

THIS IS THE FINE PRINT: ALL WHITE FISH PRESS BOOKS ARE DISTRIBUTED BY NO ONE EXCEPT *I-94: A Collection of Southwest Michigan Writers* WHICH IS DISTRIBUTED BY PARTNERS BOOK DISTRIBUTING. RETAILERS CAN CALL PARTNERS FOR ORDERING INFORMATION OR JUST TO TALK ABOUT THINGS FOR A WHILE. ALL COPYRIGHTS OF THE WORK INCLUDED IN ISSUES OF *Midnight Mind* REVERT BACK TO THE AUTHOR UNLESS THE AUTHOR IS FROM L'ANSE, MICHIGAN, IN WHICH CASE WE RETAIN ALL RIGHTS FOR THE REST OF TIME. WE STAND BY THE AUTHORS UNLESS YOU ARE BRINGING SUIT AGAINST THEM IN WHICH CASE WE WILL TESTIFY AGAINST NAMED AUTHOR AS LONG AS IT CLEARS OUR OWN NAME.

auschenberg exhib
oln a couple of y
my cool.
don't think that
ming to NY. I a
DC for 4 days
ust return to CA
ass again. This
ews but surely Iw
ming your way a
ometime soon. Y
lways welcome

WHERE IS YOUR NATIONAL PARK?